PRACTICAL WISDOM

RICHARD E. SIMMONS III

PRACTICAL WISDOM

The ART of LIVING WELL

Union Hill Publishing

Union Hill Publishing
200 Union Hill Drive, Suite 200
Birmingham, AL 35209

www.richardesimmons3.com

1 2 3 4 5 6 7 8 9 1 0

Printed in the United States of America

Wisdom is a rich mine
of common sense for those who live well,
it serves as a personal bodyguard.

Proverbs 2:7

Table of Contents

Preface

SEVERAL YEARS AGO, I read an enlightening excerpt from the great Roman philosopher and statesman, Seneca. He was born in 4 B.C. and wrote about wisdom in one of his famous essays, "On the Happy Life." He noted that too many people wander aimlessly through life, never looking for guidance. They follow only the noise and contradictions of those who seek to have us follow them. Seneca concludes that this is what leads us into a host of problems and mistakes. And since this life is so brief, we should strive day and night for sound wisdom.

Seneca then added, "Nothing, therefore, needs to be more emphasized than the warning that we should not, like sheep, follow the lead of the throng in front of us, traveling, thus, the way that all go and not the way we ought to go."

It is important to know and understand what wisdom is, in order to understand its value. The Hebrew word for wisdom is "chokmah," and the translation is "to have a skill and expertise in living." This should cause each of us to stop and ask the question, how valuable would it be if I was an expert in living?

Furthermore, wisdom enables us to interpret the world and how we should live in it. A person who lacks wisdom lives without direction and is lost in a world that does not make sense.

The great German theologian Gerhard Von Rad has written extensively on the issue of wisdom. He described wisdom as becoming competent in regard to the realities of life. In other words, wisdom knows how life really works, and knows how things happen, and then knows what to do about it.

This book is a collection of short essays on practical wisdom. One of the definitions of the word "practical" is "an idea or plan that is likely to succeed or be effective in real world circumstances." You will find that there is much practical wisdom in each essay that can easily be applied to your life. My hope is this book serves as a guide to help you walk in wisdom on your journey toward a healthy and meaningful life.

1

Introductory Essays

1.1

Sharpening the Saw

THIRTY YEARS AGO, I wandered into a bookstore and noticed a book with an intriguing title: *The Seven Habits of Highly Effective People*, by Stephen Covey. I had never heard of the book or the author, but it went on to become one of the best-selling books of all time.

I also admit it had a profound impact on my life. I would like to discuss the seventh habit, which Covey calls "Sharpening the Saw." He begins the chapter with a great little story:

Suppose you were to come upon someone in the woods working feverishly to saw down a tree.

"What are you doing?" you ask.

"Can't you see?" comes the impatient reply. "I'm sawing down this tree."

"You look exhausted!" you exclaim. "How long have you been at it?"

"Over five hours," he returns, "and I'm beat! This is hard work."

"Well, why don't you take a break for a few minutes and sharpen that saw?" you enquire. "I'm sure it would go a lot faster."

"I don't have time to sharpen the saw," the man says emphatically. "I'm too busy sawing!"

Habit 7 is taking time to sharpen the saw. It surrounds the other habits on the Seven Habits paradigm because it is the habit that makes all the others possible.

Covey is trying to tell us that we get so busy with life that we forget to take time for personal growth and development, which makes us ineffective in the most important areas of life. For this reason, it is imperative to strengthen and enhance the greatest asset you have – *you*.

Covey goes on to say:

> *This is the single most powerful investment we can ever make in life – investment in ourselves, in the only instrument we have with which to deal with life and to contribute. We are the instruments of our own performance, and to be effective, we need to recognize the importance of taking time regularly to sharpen the saw.*
>
> *There are clearly four dimensions of life where consistent growth is needed if we are going to see our lives flourish and if we are to be healthy, balanced people.*

SPIRITUAL
RELATIONAL
MENTAL
PHYSICAL

One of the greatest truths that has become so apparent to me is that if you want to grow and develop any area of your life, you have to be intentional. You have to plan for growth or it will never happen.

My challenge to each of you reading this book is to examine the most important areas of your life, come up with a plan for growth, and then execute that plan.

This is a choice you have to make, knowing that your life will be determined by all of the choices you make over the course of time. As the legendary basketball Coach John Wooden put it: "There is a choice you have to make in everything you do. So keep in mind that in the end, the choice you make is what ultimately makes you."

1.2

The Value of Wisdom

HAVE YOU ever seen a person live recklessly on the edge until, one day, they crash into the wall of reality? It amazes me how so many people believe they can make bad choices and get away unscathed. Ultimately, these people lack wisdom.

Wisdom allows us to understand the laws and principles of life, therefore enabling us to harmonize our lives with reality. Instead of running headlong into it, we can prosper in our relationship with it. Ultimately, wisdom protects us.

Years ago, I read a simple illustration that provides great insight into the way wisdom works in our lives.

> A little girl watches her mother doing the ironing. The child is intrigued by the process as the iron eats up the wrinkles and creases in each garment. The phone rings. As the mother goes to answer it, she says to her little girl, "Don't touch that iron; it's hot." The child now has knowledge – the iron is hot. As soon as her mother disappears, the little girl decides to try her own hand at ironing. Unfortunately, she touches the iron in the wrong place and is burned. She now has understanding – the iron is hot. The next day the mother continues with the ironing and again she is summoned by the phone. Again, she issues a warning: "Don't touch the iron; it's hot." Again,

the temptation to do some ironing comes over the little girl. She puts out her hand to grab the iron. Then she remembers her burned finger and leaves the iron alone. She now has wisdom – the iron is hot.

From this simplistic story, we see how wisdom impacts the decisions we make in life. When you get right down to it, wisdom changes people. It impacts not only what you see but also your choices. At the end of the day, it is your choices that determine the ultimate outcome of your life.

It strikes me that wise people are very forward-thinking. They understand that all of life is connected. There is a cause-and-effect relationship, between the choices they make today, and what they experience tomorrow.

In Proverbs 27:12, Solomon says:

"A prudent man sees evil and hides himself, the naïve proceed and pay the penalty."

In commenting on this verse, Andy Stanley, founder of North Point Ministries, says:

Prudent people look as far down the road as possible when making decisions. Every decision. After all, they understand that today and tomorrow are connected. As the author of Proverbs states, they stay on the lookout for signs of trouble up ahead. Today's decisions are informed and influenced by their impact on tomorrow. Drawing on their own experience of the experience of others, they anticipate the future and choose accordingly. They ask, "In light of my past experience, and my future hopes and dreams, what's the wise thing to do?" The prudent draw upon the wealth of data that life has already provided them and then take appropriate action when they see danger ahead.

In contrast to the prudent, the simple or naïve person lives as though life is disconnected as if there is no connection between today's choices and tomorrow's experiences. When the simple "see danger," they don't take evasive action. They keep going.

Notice, I said they live as if life is disconnected. They don't necessarily believe that to be the case. If you were to ask them, "Do you think there is a connection between the choices you make today and what you will experience in the future?" They would in all likelihood answer, "Yes." Although they do believe life is connected, they simply don't live like it is. Their actions do not reflect their beliefs.

The 1960s was a turbulent time in our country. Young people did not like all the structure they saw in the lives of their parents. They desired to be liberated from all the restrictions that society imposed upon them. Many of them just dropped out of society and lived in communes.

In the late 1960s, a group of hippies living in the Haight-Ashbury District of San Francisco decided that hygiene was a middle-class hang-up that they best could do without. For example, baths and showers, while not actually banned, were frowned upon. The essayist and novelist Tom Wolfe was intrigued by these hippies who he said, "sought nothing less than to sweep aside all codes and restraints of the past and start out from zero." To be totally autonomous and free.

Before long, the hippies' aversion to modern hygiene had consequences that were as unpleasant as they were unforeseen. Wolfe gives this description: "At the Haight-Ashbury Free Clinic there were doctors who were treating diseases no living doctor had ever encountered before, diseases that had disappeared so long ago they had never even picked up latin names, such as the mange, the grunge, the scroff and the rot." The itching and the manginess began to vex these hippies, leading them to seek help from the local free clinics. Step by step they had to rediscover for themselves the necessity of modern hygiene.

Clearly, all of life has an underlying structure designed by God. This is why we have these universal principles that are built into life, and we violate them at our own peril.

Wisdom recognizes the importance of honoring this underlying structure. This is why Solomon says, "wisdom preserves the lives of its possessors" (Ecclesiastes 7:12).

1.3

Are My Beliefs True

HAVE YOU ever worried that some cherished belief you hold might not be true? I have been thinking a great deal lately about the importance of believing responsibly. I am not always sure we realize that when we truly believe something, the stakes are very high because our beliefs can be truly consequential, particularly if the belief is in error.

I recently read about the practice of medicine back in the eighteenth century. In those days, medical doctors were taught the time-honored practice of bloodletting to help cure sick patients by removing bad or stagnant blood. Unchallenged for more than four thousand years, bloodletting was universally accepted as the most effective remedy for almost every disease. Although it seems archaic today, the prevailing theory before the circulatory system was fully understood was that blood could stagnate in the extremities. A buildup of bad blood was thought to cause all manner of maladies. The cure was to purge.

And everyone bought in for centuries! Ancient cultures like the Mesopotamians and Egyptians. Hippocrates, the father of modern medicine, also endorsed bloodletting as an effective treatment, as did Socrates and Plato. The Talmud, the central text of Rabbinic Judaism, specified certain days for bloodletting, and early Christian writings offered advice on which saints' days were most favorable for the practice. Bloodletting was prescribed for everything from cholera to cancer, tetanus to tuber-culosis, gout to gangrene. The more blood, the better. In 1799, George Washington, suffering from a throat infection, requested that his physician drain four pints of blood. Not surprisingly, shortly after the procedure, Washington died.

It wasn't until the young scientist, Louis Pasteur discov-ered that it was germs, not bad blood that caused disease. This changed everything in the medical field. You can imagine the shock of experienced doctors when they learned that their at-tempts to heal had actually harmed or even killed their patients. This is the destructive power of believing what is false.

From this, it is crucial to understand that truth has to be discovered, it cannot be invented. Truth is an objective reality you seek to discover and understand; it never changes. It is not subject to debate or dialogue and does not evolve with time.

I truly believe that if you want to live a healthy life that is in harmony with reality, you must seek to follow the truth wherever it may lead you. This is the way of the wise.

1.4

Truth and Our Perception of Reality

A FAMOUS WRITER was in his study. He picked up his pen and began writing:

"Last year, my gallbladder was removed. I was stuck in bed due to this surgery for a long time.

The same year I reached the age of 60 and had to give up my favorite job. I had spent 30 years of my life with this publishing company.

The same year I experienced the death of my father.

In the same year, my son failed in his medical exam because he had a car accident. He had to stay in the hospital with a cast on his leg for several days. And, the destruction of the car was a second loss."

His concluding statement: "Alas! It was such a bad year!!"

When the writer's wife entered the room, she found her husband looking dejected, sad and lost in his thoughts. She carefully and surreptitiously read what he had written, silently left the room and came back shortly with another piece of paper on which she had written her summary of the year's events, placing it beside her husband's paper.

When her husband saw that she had written something in response to his account of the year's events, he read:

"Last year I finally got rid of my gallbladder which had given me many years of pain.

I turned 60 with sound health and retired from my job. Now I can utilize my time to write better and with more focus and peace.

The same year, my father, at the age of 95 without depending on anyone and without any critical conditions, met his Creator.

The same year, God blessed my son with life. My car was destroyed, but my son was alive and without permanent disability."

At the end she wrote: "This year was an immense blessing and it passed well!!"

Same incidents. Different perspectives.

Isn't it amazing how our views of reality can be so divergent? It is as if we all see the world through different lenses.

Scott Peck, in his best-selling book *The Road Less Traveled*, says our view of reality is like a map that helps us navigate the terrain of life. He says:

> If the map is true and accurate, we will generally know where we are, and if we have decided where we want to go, we will generally know how to get there. If the map is false and inaccurate, we generally will be lost.

I am continuously amazed at how many people are living with the wrong maps, and they have such a difficult time figuring out why their lives are not going well. Within the pages of this book, I will share with you how to find a better map, determine a path for your life, and develop healthier habits along the way.

2

Wisdom for Growth and Development

2.1

A Plan for Personal Growth

I AM OFTEN reminded of a conversation author and speaker John Maxwell had forty years ago that radically changed his life. He was having breakfast with Kurt Kampmeir at a Holiday Inn in Lancaster, Ohio. While they were eating, Kurt posed this question:

John, what is your plan for personal growth?
Never at a loss for words, I tried to find things in my life that might qualify for growth. I told him about the many activities that I was engaged in throughout the week. I went into a speech about how hard I had worked and the gains I was making in my organization. I must have talked for ten minutes, until I finally ran out of gas. Kurt listened patiently, but then he finally smiled and said, "You don't have a personal plan for growth, do you?"

"No," I finally admitted.

"You know," Kurt said simply, "growth is not an automatic process."

Maxwell realized that, in order to grow, you have to have a plan for growth.

Last year, I turned 70, and it has been a time of deep reflection for me as I am living in the fourth quarter of life. One of the great truths that has become apparent to me is if you really want to grow and develop any area of your life, you must be intentional. You have to have a plan for growth or it will never happen. This is true in your spiritual life, marriage, career, finances, and your intellectual life.

The problem is that most people never come to understand this idea. It explains why for so many people there is a great gap between the life they aspire to lead and the one they are actually living. It explains why so many adults live with such great disappointment.

Several years ago, I encountered a principle regarding personal growth that has powerfully impacted my own life. It is called the *Vector Principle*, and I first read about it in Jerry Foster's book, *Life Focus*.

Vector, a term in mathematics and physics, quantifies the speed and direction of an object. If you were the pilot of a jetliner, you would use vectors to define the course to your destination. When you are given a new vector by the control center, you turn the plane to line up with that heading on the compass, thus creating a new vector angle.

Obviously, even the smallest vector change in the cockpit can make a big difference in the plane's ultimate destination. Though it may seem an imperceptible change, with every mile traveled you are farther from your previous course. For example, upon leaving New York, you could make a tiny vector change while flying to reach Seattle, yet you could end up in Los Angeles instead.

The Vector Principle applies to our lives in the same manner. Even if you never fly an airplane, you are vectoring through life by the choices you make. You are currently on a course that was determined by choices you have made since you were aware of your capacity to choose. Many of these choices probably seem insignificant when you make them, but small changes make a big difference over time. Most people do not realize it, but the most significant achievements in life are the result of many little things done in a single, strategic direction.

Therefore, at the beginning of each year, I seek to make three or four small but relevant changes in the most strategic areas of my life. After thirty or forty days they become habits, and these habits create a ripple effect as the years go by.

I read recently that Pat Williams, former NBA coach and senior vice-president of the Orlando Magic, was having dinner with the legendary basketball coach, John Wooden. At one point during the meal, Williams asked Coach Wooden, "Coach, if you could pinpoint just one secret of success in life, what would it be?"

Coach Wooden thought about it for a minute and responded, "The closest I can come to one single secret of success is this: a lot of little things done well."

2.2

Understanding Our Habits

DO YOU have any bad habits you have a hard time breaking? I don't know anyone who intentionally plans to develop bad habits, however, they seem to make their way into our lives without us being aware of them. At least not until they start to wreak havoc in our daily lives.

Back in 2013, I wrote a book titled, *A Life of Excellence*. In the book, I share some insightful words from Dr. Tom Morris as it relates to our habits. He says:

> Good habits usually result from thoughtful, rational decision making plus personal discipline and repetition. When establishing a new habit, getting started is generally the hardest part. For example, we might start a new exercise and diet routine because we observe our bodies slowly deteriorating or we know of people our age who've suffered heart attacks. We calculate a shortfall in our retirement needs and tighten our budgets so we can direct more financial resources to our retirement accounts. As we implement these necessary changes over time, they become permanent habits in our lives, and ultimately will lead to our future well-being.
>
> Bad habits, on the other hand, are usually not the result of logical thought or careful deliberation. Frequently,

they are a result of pleasurable sensations that make us feel good. And if it results in making us feel better, then we are prone to doing it again and again. Repetition sets in and behold—a new habit has formed.

In this day and time, good feelings often have far greater power over our ability to reason. Once established, these bad habits are much more difficult to break because they are rooted in the strength of personal feelings and pleasurable sensations.

Over the years, I have wondered how people develop patterns of living that lead to such destruction in their lives. Why would anyone allow destructive habits to form and then be so helpless to overcome them?

Recently I had an "aha" moment upon reading some profound words by author James Clear. He says we value the present more than we value the future. We prefer instant gratification over delayed gratification.

He asks the question, why would someone smoke if it dramatically increases the risk of lung cancer? Why would someone overeat when they know it increases the risk of obesity and heart disease? The reason is clear, the consequences of bad habits are delayed, while the rewards are immediate.

Think about it, smoking may result in a painful death in ten years, but it reduces stress and eases nicotine cravings, now. Overeating is harmful in the long run but tastes wonderful at the moment.

With our bad habits, the immediate outcome usually feels good, but the ultimate outcome feels bad. With good habits, it is the reverse: the immediate outcome is unenjoyable, but the ultimate outcome feels good. The French economist Frédéric Bastiat explained the problem clearly when he wrote, "It almost always happens that when the immediate consequence is favorable, the later consequences are disastrous, and vice versa . . . Often, the sweeter the first fruit of a habit, the more bitter are its later fruits."

The bottom line: the price you pay for your good habits is in the present, but you pay for your bad habits in the future.

2.3

The Power
of Compounding

I BELIEVE it is vitally important to understand the power of compounding. There is a cumulative effect when a person invests small amounts of time in certain activities over an extended period. Here, I would emphasize the phrase "cumulative effect." It has applications to every area of a person's life. For example, we know there's clearly a cumulative effect if you exercise 35 to 45 minutes a day, five days a week, over a 40 year period. This consistent, disciplined activity is in stark contrast to a sedentary lifestyle over that same period of time.

It's important to note, however, that the value of physical exercise is not found in any one particular day. Exercise has a compounding effect. It's the consistent, incremental investment of time that makes a lasting difference.

It was Albert Einstein who said, "Compound interest is the most powerful force in the universe." In Darren Hardy's book *The Compound Effect*, he shares the illustration of the magic penny.

If you were given the choice of receiving $3 million in cash right now or a single penny that would double in value every day for 31 days, which would you choose? Most people would impulsively choose the $3 million in cash. But, if you chose the penny, on day five you would have 16 cents, and on day ten $5.12. After 20 days, with only 11 left, you would have $5,243.

This is when the power of compounding begins its rapid ascent. On day 31, you would have $10,737,418.24.

Pennies seem so insignificant, even when they're doubling in value for the first few days. It is only with the passage of time that a paltry penny becomes a vast amount of money. Hardy says few things are as impressive as the magic of compounding pennies, and what we don't realize is that this same compounding force is equally powerful in every area of our lives.

The cumulative effect of investing small amounts of time in carefully chosen activities over an extended period can best be understood in *The Daffodil Principle*, created by Jaroldeen Edwards.

> Several times my daughter had telephoned to say, "Mother, you must come see the daffodils before they are over." I wanted to go, but it was a two-hour drive from Laguna to Lake Arrowhead. "I will come next Tuesday," I promised, a little reluctantly, on her third call.
>
> Next Tuesday dawned cold and rainy. Still, I had promised, and so I drove there. When I finally walked into Carolyn's house and hugged and greeted my grandchildren, I said, "Forget the daffodils Carolyn! The road is invisible in the clouds and fog, and there is nothing in the world except you and these children that I want to see bad enough to drive another inch!" My daughter smiled calmly and said, "We drive in this all the time, Mother."
>
> "Well, you won't get me back on the road until it clears, and then I'm heading home!" I assured her.
>
> "I was hoping you'd take me to the garage to pick up my car."
>
> "How far will we have to drive?"
>
> "Just a few blocks," Carolyn said, "I'll drive. I'm used to this."
>
> After several minutes, I had to ask, "Where are we going? This isn't the way to the garage."

"Carolyn," I said sternly, "please turn around."

"It's all right, Mother, I promise. You will never forgive yourself if you miss this experience."

After about 20 minutes, we turned onto a small gravel road and I saw a small church. On the far side of the church, I saw a hand-lettered sign with an arrow that read, Daffodil Garden. We got out of the car and each took a child's hand, and I followed Carolyn down the path. Then, we turned a corner of the path, and I looked up and gasped. Before me lay the most glorious sight.

It looked as though someone had taken a great vat of gold and poured it over the mountain peak and its surrounding slopes. The flowers were planted in majestic, swirling patterns – great ribbons and swaths of deep orange, white, lemon yellow, salmon pink, saffron and butter yellow. Each different-colored variety was planted as a group so that it swirled and flowed like its own river with its own unique hue.

There were five acres of flowers. "But who has done it?" I asked Carolyn. "It's just one woman," Carolyn answered. "She lives on the property. That's her home." Carolyn pointed to a well-kept A-frame house that looked small and modest in the midst of all that glory. We walked up to the house. On the patio, we saw a poster. "Answers to the Questions I Know You Are Asking," was the headline on the sign.

The first answer was a simple one: 50,000 bulbs, it read. The second answer was "One at a time, by one woman. Two hands, two feet, very little brain." The third answer was "Began in 1958."

There it was, *The Daffodil Principle*. For me, that moment was a life-changing experience. I thought of this woman whom I had never met, who, more than 40 years before, had begun – one bulb at a time – to bring her vision of beauty and joy to an obscure mountaintop. Still, just planting one bulb at a time, year after year, had changed the world. This unknown woman had for-ever changed the world in which she lived, She had cre-ated something indescribable: magnificence, beauty and inspiration.

The principle her daffodil garden taught is one of the greatest principles of celebration. That is, learning to move toward our goals and desires one step at a time – ofter just one baby-step at a time– and learning to love the doing, learning to use the accumulation of time. When we multiply tiny pieces of time with small incre-ments of daily effort, we, too, will find we can accomplish magnificent things. We can change the world.

"It makes me sad in a way," I admitted to Carolyn.

"What might I have accomplished if I had thought of a wonderful goal 35 or 40 years ago and had worked away at it 'one bulb at a time' through all those years? Just think what I might have been able to achieve!"

My daughter summed up the message of the day in her usual direct way. "Start tomorrow," she said.

It's so pointless to think of the lost hours of yester-days. The way to make learning a lesson of celebration instead of a cause for regret is to only ask, "How can I put this to use today?"

How do you change the course of your life? How do you live an exceptional life? Learn to use the accumulation of time. Multi-ply tiny pieces of time with small increments of daily effort and you can accomplish magnificent things. If we do not seize and take hold of our limited time, then our days will continually be devoured by random, unproductive activities that ultimately add up to a lot of wasted time. Novelist Robert Heinlein said, "In the absence of clearly defined goals, we become strangely loyal to performing daily trivia until we become enslaved by it." Because our time is, in fact, our lives, if we waste our time, we waste our lives.

Furthermore, it is essential to grasp that if we do not invest regular amounts of time into the important activities of life, the effects of compounding can work in reverse. Neglect is like an ever-growing snowball that has a cumulative negative effect. It can lead to a vicious downward spiral, bringing tremendous pain and disappointment into our lives.

The most important areas of your life require regular deposits of time as the years go by. If you miss these opportunities, they are lost forever.

2.4

Continuous Improvement

RECENTLY, I READ a true story in James Clear's book, *Atomic Habits*. In the book, he tells of the remarkable transformation of the British Cycling team. They had recently hired Dave Brailsford as their new performance director. At the time, professional cyclists in Great Britain had endured nearly one hundred years of mediocrity. Since 1908, British riders had won just a single gold medal at the Olympic games, and they had fared even worse in cycling's biggest race, the Tour de France. In 110 years, no British cyclist had ever won the event.

In fact, the performance of British riders had been so underwhelming that one of the top bike manufacturers in Europe refused to sell bikes to the team because they were afraid it would hurt sales if other professionals saw the Brits using their gear.

Brailsford had been hired to put British Cycling on a new trajectory. What made him different from previous coaches was his relentless commitment to a strategy that he referred to as "the aggregation of marginal gains," which was the philosophy of searching for a tiny margin of improvement in everything you do. Brailsford said, "The whole principle came from the idea that if you break down everything you could think of that goes into riding a bike, and then improve it by 1 percent, you will get a significant increase when you put them all together."

Brailsford and his coaches began by making the small adjustments you might expect from a professional cycling team. They redesigned the bike seats to make them more comfortable and rubbed alcohol on the tires for a better grip. They asked riders to wear electrically heated overshorts to maintain ideal muscle temperature while riding and used biofeedback sensors to monitor how each athlete responded to a particular workout. The team tested various fabrics in a wind tunnel and had their outdoor riders switch to indoor racing suits, which proved to be lighter and more aerodynamic.

But they didn't stop there. Brailsford and his team continued to find 1 percent improvements in overlooked and unexpected areas. They tested different types of massage gels to see which one led to the fastest muscle recovery. They hired a surgeon to teach each rider the best way to wash their hands to reduce the chances of catching a cold. They determined the type of pillow and mattress that led to the best night's sleep for each rider. They even painted the inside of the team truck white, which helped them spot little bits of dust that would normally slip by unnoticed but could degrade the performance of the finely tuned bikes.

As these and hundreds of other small improvements accumulated, the results came faster than anyone could have imagined.

Just five years after Brailsford took over, the British Cycling team dominated the road and track cycling events at the 2008 Olympic Games in Beijing, where they won an astounding 60 percent of the gold medals available. Four years later, when the Olympic Games came to London, the Brits raised the bar as they set nine Olympic records and seven world records.

That same year, Bradley Wiggins became the first British cyclist to win the Tour de France. The next year, his teammate Chris Froome won the race, and he would go on to win again in 2015, 2016, and 2017, giving the British team five Tour de France victories in six years.

During the ten-year span from 2007 to 2017, British cyclists won 178 world championships and 66 Olympic or Paralympic gold medals and captured 5 Tour de France victories in what is widely regarded as the most successful run in cycling history.

Obviously, every cycling team that competes in the Olympics wants to win a medal, particularly the gold medal. However, it strikes me that simply having a goal does not differentiate those who win from those who lose. Just having a goal does not propel you to a successful outcome. Throughout their history, the British Cycling teams always wanted to win their events. It wasn't until they implemented this system of small, continuous improvements that they were able to actually achieve a successful outcome. Therefore, I encourage you to look at all the different areas of your life and strategically search for small changes that will have a significant impact over time. It may require you to think outside of the box to find where these small improvements may be, but this can truly be life-changing.

I leave you with this wonderful quote from Carl Richards: "Micro-actions, done repeatedly over a very long time, compound into massive results."

2.5

The Art
of Achieving

I RECENTLY READ an interesting book titled *Flourish*. It was written by the prominent psychologist Martin Seligman who teaches at the University of Pennsylvania.

In the book, he says the basic equation to growth, development, and achievement (in any area of life) is based on your skill and ability, multiplied by the effort you expend. He defines effort as the time you are willing to spend on a task.

Seligman then looks to the findings of Dr. Anders Ericsson, a professor of psychology at Florida State.

Ericsson has argued that the cornerstone of all high expertise is not God-given genius but deliberate practice: Mozart was Mozart not primarily because he had a unique gift for music but because from toddlerhood, he spent all his time using his gift. World-class chess players are not faster of thought, nor do they have unusually good memories for moves. Rather, they have so much experience that they are vastly better at recognizing patterns in chess positions than lesser chess players – and this comes from the sheer amount of their experience.

Seligman then makes an interesting observation about the time we are willing to devote to growth and achievement. He says it has to do with our character. Self-discipline is the character trait that engenders deliberate practice. Self-discipline is defined as the ability to make yourself do something you don't necessarily want to do to get a result you would really like to have.

He then shares some very interesting research on self-discipline with the students of Mastermind High School, in Philadelphia. Mastermind accepts promising students beginning in the fifth grade, though many of them wash out and the real competition begins in the ninth grade. The researchers studied a group of eighth graders to find out how self-discipline compares with IQ in predicting academic achievement.

They employed a battery of tests to determine which students possessed the character trait of self-discipline. For instance, they looked at how well the students could delay gratification. Therefore, they might ask, "Would you rather I give you five dollars today or ten dollars in two weeks?"

They then studied the highly self-disciplined eighth graders and found they:

- Earned higher grade point averages
- Had higher achievement test scores
- Spent more time on their homework and started it earlier in the day,
- Were absent less often
- Watched less television

In the end, the research concluded that self-discipline outpredicts IQ for academic success by a factor of about two. Whenever we underachieve in any area of life, we look for something or someone to blame. In reality, the reason is an unwillingness to sacrifice short-term pleasure for long-term gain.

Seligman believes his findings apply to every area of our lives, without exception.

3

Wisdom for Finance

3.1

Financial Wisdom

ONE OF THE best books ever written on personal finance, in my opinion, is *The Millionaire Next Door*, by Dr. Thomas Stanley and Dr. William Danko. It was published more than 20 years ago, making its "millionaire" of the past worth around two to three million dollars today.

The book opens with an intriguing scenario:

These people cannot be millionaires! They don't look like millionaires, they don't dress like millionaires, they don't eat like millionaires, they don't act like millionaires — they don't even have millionaire names. Where are the millionaires who look like millionaires?

The person who said this was a vice president of a trust department. He made these comments following a focus group interview and dinner that we hosted for 10 first-generation millionaires. His view of millionaires is shared by most people who are not wealthy. They think millionaires own expensive clothes, watches and other status artifacts. We have found this not to be the case.

As a matter of fact, our trust officer friend spends significantly more for his suits than the typical American millionaire. He also wears a $5,000 watch. We know from our surveys that the majority of millionaires never spent even one-tenth of $5,000 for a watch. Our friend also drives a current-model imported luxury car. Most millionaires are not driving this year's model. Only a minority drive a foreign motor vehicle. An even smaller minority drive foreign luxury cars. Our trust officer leases, while only a minority of millionaires ever lease their motor vehicles.

But, ask the typical American adult this question: Who looks more like a millionaire? Would it be our friend, the trust officer, or one of the people who participated in our interview? We would wager that most people by a wide margin would pick the trust officer. But, looks can be deceiving.

Drs. Stanley and Danko spent 20 years studying the lives of the affluent before they published their findings. They began by surveying those who lived in upscale neighborhoods throughout the country. Over time, they discovered many of the people who live in expensive homes and drive fancy cars do not have much wealth. Even so, many people who do have a great deal of wealth do not live in upscale neighborhoods.

The researchers recognized that people have allowed themselves to be deceived. They have all the wrong ideas about building wealth; having a big income is not the same as being wealthy. If a family has a large income, but spends it all every year, they are not building wealth, they are living lavishly. People seem to have a hard time understanding that wealth is what you accumulate, not what you spend.

The most perplexing question in my mind is, "How is it that so many people who make a great deal of money and live lavish lifestyles are flat-broke?" They have little or no net worth other than maybe the equity in their homes. What would cause someone to live so foolishly and not make better decisions? Undoubtedly, just about everyone likes nice things and could enjoy a high-end lifestyle, but there is a deeper issue involved that you may not be aware of.

In 1899, economist Thorstein Veblen wrote the book, *The Theory of the Leisure Class.* Veblen coined a special term describing many upper-income Americans.

Conspicuous Consumption

This is when you buy something, not primarily for its usefulness, but for the way it makes you look in the eyes of others. Veblen shared the following message 118 years ago:

> People above the line of base subsistence, in this age and all earlier ages, do not use the surplus, which society has given them, primarily for useful purposes. They do not seek to expand their own lives, to live more wisely, intelligently, understandingly, but to impress other people with the fact that they have a surplus . . . spending money, time and effort quite uselessly in the pleasurable business of inflating the ego.

Though we may not realize it, there is a psychological fulfillment that comes from being envied by others. Veblen contended that it is possible to persuade people to buy products that are not particularly superior in quality by publicizing widely that the products are expensive.

This is how he came up with the term conspicuous consumption. People buy costly items, not because they are higher quality, but because the possession displays to others how rich the owners are.

Veblen expresses we often make purchases to make a statement to the world that we are wealthy. Furthermore, in this modern culture of easy credit, men and women accumulate enormous debt just to live lavishly and keep up with the Joneses.

It is amazing how we allow the opinions of others to influence the decisions we make and how we choose to live our lives. This illustrates how people with high incomes can become conspicuous consumers and have little to show for it at the end of the day.

3.2

The Root of
Financial Problems

SEVERAL YEARS AGO, I performed a study on money and finance, and ran across some noteworthy remarks by King David:

> "He has dug a pit and hollowed it out, and has fallen into the hole, which he made" (Psalms 7:15).

This is what often happens to people with their finances. They dig a deep financial hole, generally because they incur too much debt, and then they fall into the hole.

In the book of Proverbs, we read that the wise person understands his ways and carefully considers his steps, particularly as they relate to finances (Proverbs 14:8,15). On the other hand, a fool is out of touch with reality. As I mentioned in earlier chapters, fools are not forward-thinking, and, therefore, do not give much thought to financial planning, running up large amounts of debt instead.

Not long ago, a young man visited my office, seeking advice. Though I didn't know him very well, he appeared to be successful based on the upscale neighborhood he lived in and the lifestyle he led.

I quickly learned that his marriage was in trouble and that he was experiencing incredible financial pressure. He had maxed out all his lines of credit, had no equity in his house, and was struggling just to pay the mortgage. Finally, he told me that selling his house and downsizing was not an option because his wife refused to move out of their popular neighborhood.

I could not help him because he was not in touch with reality. Over a 10-year period, he had dug a financial hole, fallen into it, and did not know how to get out. It struck me how money has such a deceptive power. It blinds us in such a way that we make terrible financial decisions.

I find most financial problems to be the result of too much debt. Like King David, Solomon addresses debt in the book of Proverbs.

> The rich rule over the poor, and the borrower becomes the lender's slave. (Proverbs 22:7)
>
> Do not be among those who give pledges, among those who become guarantors for debts. If you have nothing with which to pay, why should he take your bed from under you? (Proverbs 22:26,27)

I feel it is clear that debt is not sinful, but the Bible discourages it when it is not necessary. The main reason is because lenders have power over the borrower. I remember a very wise older man once said to me, "If you don't go into debt, you will never go bankrupt."

A good question we should consider is, "When is it wise to go into debt and when is it not? What is a good reason to go into debt and what is not?"

A majority of financial advisors would agree that a mortgage on your house or a loan on a car is reasonable because the loan is backed by an asset that can be disposed of rather quickly to pay it off.

Additionally, one of the greatest accumulators of debt today is from student loans and education. While this, too, is reasonable and necessary for the future success of many young people, I caution them to not put off paying these debts or spend large sums of money on unnecessary things until they are able to pay off these loans.

Sound bankers make good loans that make sense, and they do it to protect the bank while protecting the borrower as well. It is when lending institutions throw their standards out the window that they get in trouble, as do the borrowers. This is what happened in the last financial crisis.

Greg Brenneman is one of the world's leading business turnaround executives. In his book, *Right Away and All at Once*, he shares wise words on debt. He says we should always match our debts with the life of our assets. There is a reason your credit card bills come due every 30 days, your car loan in five years, and most home mortgages in 30 years. These loans have been set up to match the life of the underlying asset. Groceries and a tank of gasoline last less than a month, automobiles last five years or more, and homes much longer.

Where people get in trouble is by borrowing to support lavish lifestyles with items such as jewelry, designer clothes, and vacations. This is generally done through credit card debt, and when this happens, many begin digging a hole that will prove more difficult to climb out of than it was to dig in the first place.

Michael Kidwell and Steve Rhode, authors of *Get Out of Debt: Smart Solutions to Your Money Problems*, share this:

> Debt is one of the leading causes of divorce, lack of sleep and poor work performance. It is truly one of the deep, dark secrets that people have. It robs them of their self-worth and keeps them from achieving dreams.

It is quite clear that being debt-free is a wise objective. When a person is out of debt, he or she discovers their possessions and lifestyle no longer possess them.

3.3

The Psychology of Money

SEVERAL WEEKS ago, I read a review in *The Wall Street Journal* on a book titled, *The Psychology of Money* by Morgan Housel. It was a good review, and while I thought it might be an interesting read, I ended up not purchasing it. Coincidentally, one week later, a friend gifted me a copy and left it for me on my desk. As it turns out, it is an excellent read and full of wisdom.

One chapter of the book focuses on why so many people have inadequate financial resources, particularly for retirement. Housel says:

> Spending beyond a pretty low level of materialism is mostly a reflection of ego approaching income, a way to spend money to show people that you have (or had) money.
>
> Think of it like this, one of the most powerful ways to increase your savings isn't to raise your income. It's to raise your humility.
>
> When you define savings as the gap between your ego and your income you realize why many people with decent incomes save so little. It's a daily struggle against instincts to extend your peacock feathers to their outermost limits and keep up with others doing the same.

People with enduring personal finance success—not necessarily those with high incomes—tend to have a propensity to not give a damn what others think about them.

Housel goes on to say savings are created by less spending, which occurs when people desire less. He then concludes that you will want less if you care less about what others think of you. This is why he believes our financial lives are primarily influenced by psychological forces.

I, however, would go deeper. I believe we are talking more about issues of the heart: particularly pride. Here, I would define pride as a form of arrogance and a desire to be superior to others. Pride is what causes us to seek to impress.

In Mathew 23:5, we are told the scribes and Pharisees "do all of their deeds to be noticed by men." Their lives are driven to win the approval of man.

C.S. Lewis calls pride, "the great sin." He says it is a spiritual cancer that prevents us from being content with what we have. It is purely spiritual and far more subtle and deadly than all other sins. We readily recognize it and hate it in others but cannot see it in our own lives.

To dig even deeper in understanding ourselves, we need to recognize that we are haunted by a deep fear that our lives don't matter. Tim Keller says the worst thing for a human being is not being disliked or vilified, but being ignored and considered insignificant. We fear being unimportant. We fear that at the end of the day, our lives won't matter to the people around us or be seen as meaningful. This is why the human heart in its deepest recesses is always seeking self-glorification.

I think this explains why there is a real and fundamental instability in our hearts: it is so easy to feel small and insignificant. As a result, we constantly look for ways to convince the world and ourselves that we matter and that our lives are important. What better way to do that than to live a lavish lifestyle that impresses others?

It becomes an unending quest to prove to the world that our lives have significance.

We will never find peace and contentment in this life until we come to terms with this conundrum. The ultimate solution is humility. The humble are continually at peace with who they are in the eyes of others. They are content with their position in life and what they possess. The humble are the only ones who are delivered from this great drive to prove to the world that "I am important!"

3.4

How Much Is Enough?

I RECENTLY TAUGHT a series on Financial Wisdom. Part of the series addressed the deceptiveness of riches, and one way that money often deceives us is by fostering the false belief that "more is always better."

The University of Michigan does an important consumer confidence survey every month, so important that it has become a key economic indicator in our country.

Several years ago, they asked, what one thing do you need to make your life better and improve its quality? The number one answer—more money. Not better relationships with God, family, or friends, not more free time, and not even their health.

Money.

Numerous individuals would contend that King Solomon was the richest man to ever live, exhibiting staggering wealth. As one commentator put it, "Solomon made Bill Gates look like a second-class citizen."

Solomon's philosophical writings in the book of Ecclesiastes offer fascinating perspectives on money that I believe to be valuable.

First, he reflects on the day he will have to leave all the fruit of his labor to someone else, asking: "Who knows whether he will be a wise man or a fool?" (Ecclesiastes 2:19)

Solomon laments the notion that, eventually, someone else will have total control over the wealth resulting from his labor and toil.

An interesting article was published in the June 17, 2015 edition of *Time* magazine titled, "70% of Rich Families Lose Their Wealth by the Second Generation." The article highlights how poorly prepared the second generation is at handling the wealth passed down to it. As one financial consultant put it, "Most of them have no clue as to the value of money . . ." The article also points out that the third generation is usually financially doomed.

Knowing this, you can see why Solomon was depressed over the thought of leaving his hard-earned estate to someone who would squander it. This leads to Solomon's second perspective on money: *"Whoever loves money never has money enough"* (Ecclesiastes 5:10)

This seems to be a natural part of the human condition: there is never enough and we always want more.

Ron Blue is a Christian financial consultant who has supported a missionary organization in Africa working with people living in abject poverty. One year, Blue visited one of the missionaries to observe his work, asking, "What is the greatest barrier among these people that keeps you from impacting their lives? Without hesitation, the missionary responded, "Materialism."

Blue was dumbfounded, as all he could see was extreme impoverishment. "How can that be?" Blue asked.

The missionary replied,

"If a man has a manure hut, he wants a mud hut. If he has a mud hut, he wants a stone hut. If his hut has a thatched roof, he wants a tin roof. If he has one cow, he wants two cows. If he has one wife, he wants two wives, and so on and so on."

Blue recognized, as did Solomon, that materialism is not about things. It is about the heart and the insatiable desire for more.

According to a 2019 study by The Vision Council surveying 2,000 Americans, 50% of participants classified themselves as workaholics. In a 2018 article by *Business Insider,* "11 American Work Habits Other Countries Avoid at All Costs," the habits of American work culture are compared to those of other nations worldwide. It states that Americans work longer, take fewer breaks and vacation days, and even socialize less while working than workers in other countries do. This is yet another example of how money creates this mentality that more is better, and it has profound effects on our daily lives.

Solomon made a third observation about wealth stating, "Whoever loves wealth is never satisfied with his income." In other words, the fruit of our labor does not satisfy us entirely and cannot fill the emptiness of life.

A perfect example that proves this theory involves studies conducted on people who win lotteries. The winners always experience a surge of euphoria when they learn of their winnings. However, in almost every situation, within six months, those same people return to the same level of satisfaction they experienced before the lottery win.

I am sure you may be thinking you would be an exception to the rule, but consider this:

Money and wealth cannot purchase a ...

1. Strong Relationship with God
2. Good marriage
3. Meaningful family life
4. Friendship
5. Wisdom
6. Peace and contentment in your soul

The bottom line is this – money and wealth cannot purchase the true riches of life.

4

Wisdom for Work-Life and Career

4.1

Business Wisdom

SEVERAL YEARS AGO, I met with a very bright business consultant from out of town. We have a mutual friend who helped set up the meeting. At a certain point during our visit, the consultant asked me if I knew of any companies in our community that might be able to use his services. Before responding, I asked him what set him and his firm apart from all the many consulting firms that were competing in the marketplace. I must tell you, I was impressed with his answer.

He told me in order to be a really successful business, there are two essential components.

First, you have to be smart. In other words, you want to have a good business strategy, state-of-the-art technology, and great marketing. You need to be well-capitalized, have a strong sales function, and also have a few remaining ingredients that lead to success.

Then secondly, he said, you have to be a healthy company. You want high morale, a real sense of unity, good communication, minimum politics, and a low turnover rate among employees.

He then explained that most companies and consulting firms focus on being smart, but his firm spends its time helping companies to become healthy.

From my experience in the business world and counseling businessmen, these words ring true. It is quite natural to try and create a smart, well-run business, but in the process fail to pay sufficient attention to the health of your company and the relationships that exist among the employees.

Philip Yancey tells the story of one of his good friends who worked as a consultant in the corporate world. At a certain point, he took some time to evaluate all the courses that he had taken and taught on the principles of good leadership and management. It occurred to him that he had never taken a course on how to love, even though the Bible presents it as the primary command in life. So he gathered a group of people and asked them to think about one question: "When have I felt loved?"

The responses included:

> When someone listens attentively to me, when someone makes me feel important, when someone encourages me, when someone respectfully challenges me, when someone cares for me when I am hurting, or when somebody gives me an unexpected gift.

Yancey's friend then decided to take some of his clients through this same exercise. One female executive in a dysfunctional company decided to put the principles into practice. Although her company discouraged fraternizing, this woman started going down the hall and stopping in offices to visit her employees. She had no real agenda for any visit. The first person was terrified, thinking she had come into his office to fire him. "No, no," she said, "I just figured that after three years of working together, I should get to know you."

She spent time with all thirteen of her employees until, one day, her boss called her in. "I don't know what the hell you're doing," he said, "but this company was almost bankrupt. It has turned around, and when I asked our people what had happened, everybody said that you were responsible."

This reminds me of what someone once told me long ago:

Your employees will be completely committed to you and the mission of the company if they know you truly care for them.

I don't know about you, but my instincts tell me that to be an exceptional organization, you clearly have to be smart, but maybe even more importantly, you have to be healthy.

4.2

Why Leaders
Fail

STEPHEN COVEY often spoke of how leadership development has changed. He said that all the relevant literature on leadership written from 1776 to 1925 emphasized the importance of character. It focused on "The Character Ethic" as the foundation of success, with emphasis on character traits such as humility, integrity, fidelity, and courage. Covey says that the character ethic "taught that there are basic principles of effective living, and that people can only experience true success and enduring happiness as they learn and integrate these principles into their basic character."

He then began to notice a shift in the literature about leadership and success. He says, "I began to feel more and more that much of the success literature of the past 50 years was superficial. It was filled with social image consciousness, techniques and quick fixes."

I believe we are seeing how the loss of this "character ethic" as Covey calls it, is playing out in the lives of the business and political leaders today.

Several years ago, an article appeared in the *Harvard Business Review* on why leaders in various business organizations fail. The core data came from a study that revealed the four primary factors that brought about the failures of those senior leaders:

- They were **authoritarian** – controlling, demanding, and not listening to others
- They were **autonomous** – little accountability, aloof, and isolated
- They committed **adultery**
- They became more and more **arrogant**

I believe the underlying reason these leaders encountered failure could be summed up by these words from the study: feeling and acting as if they were superior to all others. If you think you are superior to all others in your organization, you will find yourself believing you can treat people however you want, sleep with whomever you choose, and spend the organization's money at will. Basically, you believe you can do whatever you want and that the rules do not apply to you.

This is what arrogance does to a person's life: it makes people weak and ineffective leaders. What makes it so devastating is that arrogant people are not aware of their arrogance. Others see it clearly and are repelled by it, but an arrogant person is totally blind to it.

A number of years ago, Jim Collins, a faculty member at the Stanford University Graduate School of Business, wrote a best-selling book titled *Built to Last*. It was based on a management study of companies he and his associates performed back in the 1990s with the intent of analyzing and demonstrating how great companies sustain themselves over time.

In studying the data, Collins came up with the idea of trying to determine if certain universal characteristics distinguished truly great companies. Using tough benchmarks, Collins and his research team identified eleven elite companies that were doing a good job and which, for some reason, produced phenomenal results for fifteen consecutive years (some of these companies included Abbott Labs, Kimberly Clark, and Nucor Steel). He and his team then sought to determine how these companies made the leap from being good companies to being great companies.

He took the results of all this intensive research and wrote what would come to be one of the best-selling business books ever published, *Good to Great.*

What I find interesting is that Collins said he gave his research team explicit instructions to downplay the role of top executives. He did not believe that the business community needed another book on leadership. Although he had insisted they ignore the role of the company executives, the research team kept pushing back. They soon came to recognize something very unusual about the executives in these good-to-great companies.

They went back and forth until, as Collins put it, "the data won." They recognized that all the executives from these good-to-great companies were cut from the same cloth. They all were what he called "Level 5 Leaders."

Collins wrote, "Level 5 Leaders are a study in duality: modest and willful, humble and fearless." These good-to-great leaders never desired to be celebrities or to be lifted up on a pedestal. Collins declared that they were "seemingly ordinary people quietly producing extraordinary results." What Collins and his team of researchers clearly observed is that a Level 5 Leader builds enduring greatness through the paradoxical blend of personal humility and professional will. For this reason, I truly believe the greatest character trait a leader can possess is humility.

4.3

Finding Purpose in Our Work

ONE OF the wisest men I know once told me that a person's perspective is of critical importance because it can change the way we see the world. It impacts our priorities and the way we approach life. He told me that if you want to see long-term change in a person's life, you must first change their perspective.

One of the world's great architects was a man by the name of Christopher Wren. He designed St. Paul's Cathedral in London which was built between 1675 and 1710. During construction, everything was performed by human labor since there was no machinery or equipment to assist them with their work. There were hundreds of workers on the job.

One day, Wren was examining the job site where the workers were grinding away at their laborious task. There was nothing enjoyable about it. Suddenly, Wren noticed an older man who was mixing cement in a mortar box. The man seemed to be enjoying his work; he had a smile on his face. As he watched this man mix the mortar, he finally asked him, "Mister, what are you doing?" The man replied, "Sir, I am building a great cathedral to the glory of God."

I am sure that most of the men working on the cathedral saw their work as drudgery and considered it as nothing more than a way to make a living. However, this older man had a completely different experience because of his perspective.

He saw himself engaged in a noble task of great signifi-cance and it changed everything.

For many people, in order to find purpose in their work, they have to change their perspective. Dr. Tom Morris shares a great example of this in his book, *The Art of Achievement.* He tells the story of Nick Campbell, an engineer with Johnson & Johnson, who found his work to be pure drudgery.

He was working entirely for himself, thinking only about what was good for his career, but he wasn't getting the rewards or promotions he so desperately wanted. Every day was full of frustration. He hated Monday mornings for days in advance. Coworkers even called him "B.A." for "bad attitude."

When he was twenty-nine, back surgery took him out of the fray and gave him time to stop and think about his life, his attitude, and his mental approach to work. He came to realize that what he had been doing had not been working, and so he would have to change. Reading some of the best business and motivational literature, he began to understand the role of atti-tude and inner visions for outer success. As a result, he decided to use his imagination to envision his work in a whole new way, and that inner change made more of a difference than he ever could have imagined.

Nick began to think of himself as working for Campbell, Inc.—a wholly-owned subsidiary of Johnson & Johnson. He took emotional ownership of the equipment in the lab, check-ing it at the end of the day to make sure it was clean and ready for the next morning. He then decided to see himself as being in the customer service business and to view all of his associates as his customers. If he could help them solve their problems, he would have a successful day.

He started coming to work with a completely different at-titude of expectant challenge, helpfulness, and emotional in-vestment. Uncoincidentally, he started enjoying his work for the first time ever. People soon were thanking him for what he was doing. He was feeling a new pride in each day's work. In the midst of this, he was summoned to his supervisor's office. At first, he worried that perhaps he was being perceived as taking too much time from his primary assignments in his efforts to help solve others' problems, but there was no cause for anxiety. Because of what he was accomplishing for the whole department, and in recognition of his new level of commitment, Nick was promoted two levels. The prize that had eluded him when he sought it directly now was being handed to him for what he was accomplishing in service to the other people around him.

Nick Campbell's life and career were transformed when he developed a new perspective, which led to more creative thinking and a new sense of purpose in what he was doing.

Barbara Glanz is a motivational speaker and tells a wonderful story. It was at an event where she addressed three thousand frontline workers for a grocery store chain.

Barbara was speaking on how people can make a difference. She described how every interaction with another person is a chance to create a memory, to bless someone's life. She talked about how important it is to look for those moments.

After she finished her speech, she left her phone number and invited the people at the conference to give her a call if they wanted to discuss more about something she had said.

About a month later, Barbara received a call from one of the people at that session, a nineteen-year-old bagger named Johnny. Johnny proudly informed her he had Down syndrome and then he told her his story.

"Barbara, I liked what you talked about. But I didn't think I could do anything special for our customers. After all I'm just a bagger."

Then he had an idea: he decided that every night when he came home from work, he would find a "thought for the day" for his next shift. It would be something positive, some reminder of how good it was to be alive, or how much people matter, or how many gifts we are surrounded by. If he couldn't find one, he would make one up.

Every night, his dad would help him enter the saying six times on a page on the computer; Johnny would print fifty pages. He would take out a pair of scissors and carefully cut three hundred copies and sign each one.

Johnny put the stack of pages next to him while he worked. Each time he finished bagging someone's groceries, he would put his saying on top of the last bag. Then, he would stop what he was doing, look the person straight in the eye, and say, "I've put a great saying in your bag. I hope it helps you have a good day. Thanks for coming here." A month later, the store manager called Barbara.

"Barbara, you won't believe what's happened here. I was making my rounds, and when I got up to the cashiers, the line at Johnny's checkout was three times longer than anyone else's. It went all the way down the frozen food aisle."

The manager got on the loudspeaker to get more checkout lines open, but he couldn't get any of the customers to move. They said, "That's okay. We'll wait. We want to be in Johnny's line." One woman came up to him and grabbed his hand, saying, "I used to shop in your store once a week. Now I come in every time I go by – I want to get Johnny's thought for the day." Johnny is doing more than filling bags with groceries; he is filling lives with hope. He is touching people's lives

Most of us probably do not think that bagging groceries could be a purposeful occupation. However, once Johnny realized that he could bless and encourage others, his job which seemed so unimportant became quite significant.

4.4

Finding Passion in Our Work

RECENTLY, I READ about an interesting study published in Mark Albion's book, *Making a Life, Making a Living*. The study is very revealing in that it examines businesspeople who took very different paths after graduating from college.

A study of business school graduates tracked the careers of 1,500 people from 1960 to 1980. From the beginning, the graduates were grouped into two categories. Category A consisted of people who said they wanted to make money first so that they could do what they really wanted to do later – after they had taken care of their financial concerns. Those in Category B pursued their true interests first, sure that the money would eventually follow.

What percentage fell into each category?

Of the 1,500 graduates in the survey, the money-now Category A's comprised 83 percent, or 1,245 people. Category B risk takers made up 17 percent or 255 graduates. After twenty years there were 101 millionaires in the group. One came from Category A. One hundred came from Category B.

The study's author, Srully Blotnick, concluded that "the overwhelming majority of people who have become wealthy have become so thanks to work they found pro-foundly absorbing. . . . Their 'luck' arose from the acci-dental dedication they had to an area they enjoyed."

I believe this study could be of great value to a college gradu-ate or people in their early thirties as they consider their future careers. But, what about the person who has already invested twenty or twenty-five years in a career in which they are bored or even miserable?

Over the years, I have asked many people the following question: "What if you just learned that your long-lost uncle had died and left you enough money so you would never have to work again? What would you do tomorrow?" A few have told me they would stay the course and make no changes in their lives. Many have told me they would scale down and take a less stressful position. However, a large majority said, "I would turn in my resignation tomorrow."

The problem is many believe they cannot change careers because they earn a good living and have built up a lifestyle they are not willing to walk away from. So many people find themselves in an unprecedented place—being incredibly well educated, with a world full of options for meaningful work, and yet, they have no idea where they belong.

So, what do you tell this person?

First, you may want to change careers. I am not suggest-ing you resign tomorrow but go ahead and make the decision that you are going to find a more meaningful career. Make the change once you have determined what that is or wait until you have actually found another job. As someone once said, "When Tarzan is swinging through the jungle, he never lets go of the first vine until he has his hand firmly attached to the second."

For many people it is not realistic to change careers, at least right now. It is important to know that if you are young, this is the easiest time to make that career change. However, you also need to be wise and not have a resume where you have had five jobs in ten years.

Overall, how we approach our work can be as important as the nature of the work itself. If we step back and see our work as a calling, that we are providing a service to help others, that our work connects us to people and is part of a bigger vision, it will impact what we experience in our jobs.

4.5

Failure: One of Life's Greatest Blessings

TONY CAMPOLO tells of a study done years ago by a group of sociologists. They interviewed a large number of people, and the only criteria to be chosen for the study was that you had to be at least ninety-five years old. They were asked this one question: "If you could live your life over again, what would you do differently?" One of the most common answers of this group of elderly people was, "If I could go back and live my life over again, I would have taken more risks."

What strikes me with this answer is that these people in their twilight years realized what a mistake it was to play it safe over the course of their lives because they were afraid to fail. If you think about it, most of the great accomplishments in life are the result of people willing to step out of their comfort zones into the unknown, knowing that failure is a possibility.

I have concluded that the fear of failure paralyzes most people. It is like a psychological death. Larry Crabb says that we try to arrange our lives so that everything is predictable and under our control. We pursue endeavors where we feel competent and can hide our inadequacies, avoiding what we fear and thereby creating a feeling of safety.

However, have you ever thought about how failure can be something positive? I contend it can be one of the great blessings of life, depending on how we respond to it.

I love the way the great Swiss psychologist Paul Tournier puts it:

> "Only rarely are we the masters of events," he [Tournier} says, "but (along with those who help us) we are responsible for our reactions." In other words, we are accountable for the way we respond to the struggles we encounter. Tournier believed that a positive, active, and creative response to one of life's challenges will develop us while a negative and angry one will only debilitate us and stunt our growth.

In fact, Tournier believed the right response at the right moment might actually determine the course of a person's entire life. He found that, quite often, humans are presented with rare opportunities to develop and grow through hardship and trial—particularly failure.

We need to understand how perseverance in the midst of failure shapes us as people. The best example of this I have seen is Abraham Lincoln. Lincoln tried and failed many times over the course of his political career as depicted in this timeline.

1833 – Started a business that failed.
1836 – Suffered a nervous breakdown.
1843 – Defeated for nomination to Congress.
1846 – Elected to Congress but lost nomination
         2 years later.
1854 – Defeated in attempt to win a seat in the U.S. Senate.
1856   Defeated for nomination to be Vice President.
1858 – Again, defeated in U.S. Senate race.

In 1860 he was elected President of the United States and is considered by many to have been our greatest President. It makes you wonder if he ever considered himself a failure, a loser. I cannot say for sure, but look how he persevered in the midst of defeat. This should be of great value to each of us. Though no one wants to fail, maybe when we do, it can serve a purpose as it shapes and molds us into people of strong character.

4.6

How to Be a
Student of Life

IN THE FEBRUARY 22, 2014 edition of *The New York Times*, there was a fascinating article by Thomas Friedman entitled, "How to Get a Job at Google." It was written from an interview with Laszlo Bock, the senior vice president in charge of hiring at Google, one of the world's most successful companies.

In the hiring process, Bock says, "GPAs are worthless as a criterion for hiring and test scores are worthless; we found they don't predict anything." He then proceeds to share what they are looking for in the prospective new hires that come to interview with Google. One of the primary attributes they desire is humility. They are looking for courageous leaders who, at the appropriate times, will step up and lead, but who will also be willing to relinquish power when needed. In other words, they need to be humble enough to step back and embrace the better ideas of others.

Bock also stressed the importance of having intellectual humility, for if you do not have this, you will be unable to learn even from failure. Too many proud people believe they are a genius when something good happens, but when something bad happens, it is someone else's fault.

Google seems to understand that truly humble people are what Jim Collins called, "a study in duality: modest and willful, humble and fearless." Bock declares that they are looking for people to take firm positions and who will argue like hell. However, when they learn a new fact, they need to let go of their ego and be willing to change their point of view.

Bock recognizes that in an age of innovation, their work is increasingly a group endeavor. In order to work well and effectively in the group, you have to be humble.

This is in line with something I read in Ryan Holiday's book *Ego is the Enemy*. The nine-time Grammy and Pulitzer Prize-winning jazz musician Wynton Marsalis offered this advice to a promising young musician on the mindset required to become a great musician:

> Humility engenders learning because it beats back the arrogance that puts blinders on. It leaves you open for truths to reveal themselves. You don't stand in your own way . . . Do you know how you can tell if someone is truly humble? I believe there's one simple test: because they consistently observe and listen, the humble improve. They don't assume, 'I know the way.'

Holiday says that humble people are students for life, seeking to learn from everyone and everything. It might be from people you beat or from those who have beaten you. Wherever you are in your life journey, there are opportunities to learn. This is the perspective humility brings into your life.

4.7

The Wisdom of Charlie Munger

MANY OF YOU are likely familiar with the name Charlie Munger, but in case you are not, he was the vice-chairman of Berkshire Hathaway and died recently at the age of 99. Warren Buffet refers to him as "my partner." I might add that Buffet believes Munger is one of the wisest, most knowledgeable people he ever knew.

I recently had the opportunity to read the commencement address Munger delivered at Harvard University back in 1986, and then the commencement address he delivered at the University of Southern California's (USC) School of Law in 2007.

Both addresses were quite humorous and full of sound wisdom. I would like to share several of his ideas that might be of value to you. It would be particularly valuable for younger people who have their entire lives in front of them.

In the Harvard address, the theme was "Prescriptions for Misery." He told these students how to guarantee them a miserable life as an adult. Just follow this prescription.

The heart of this talk can be summarized as follows: if you want to be miserable in life, be unreliable. It is the best way to sabotage your life, your relationships, and your career.

Munger says if you master this one habit, being unreliable, it will override all your other virtues, however great they may be. He says it is the best way to be distrusted and excluded. He says if you can master this habit, you will even be surpassed by those who are mediocre.

To master this habit, don't be on time, don't meet deadlines, fail to honor your commitments, and by all means, do not do what you say you are going to do.

Munger closes this thought by saying it is hard to be miserable if you are responsible, even if you have certain disadvantages in your life. He then references his roommate in college who was severely dyslexic. However, Munger said "he is perhaps the most reliable person I have ever known. He has had a wonderful life so far, outstanding wife and children, chief executive of a multibillion-dollar corporation."

So, if you are trying to figure out how to be miserable in life, be irresponsible.

A great example of what true reliability was in the news several years ago. It took place here, in the suburbs of Birmingham, Alabama.

Back on July 12, 2018, twenty-year-old Walter Carr, a Homewood resident who attended Lawson State and who one day hoped to join the Marines, started to have car trouble. The next day was to be the first day of his new job with Bellhops Movers. He was scheduled to be at work at 8:00 am to help move a family into their new home.

He tried to call some friends to see if he could arrange transportation but to no avail. It was getting close to midnight, and it looked as if he would not be able to make it to the job site the next morning.

However, this new job was important to him, and he did not want to let down his new employer. He had assured them he would be there at 8:00 a.m. sharp.

He pulled up his Google Maps to see how long it would take him if he walked—7 hours. He started walking at midnight from near the Palisades at Homewood to his job at the far end of Pelham, over 20 miles away. He got on US 280 and walked all night.

He was questioned by several police officers wondering why he was walking all alone in the middle of the night. After hearing his story, the policemen took him to breakfast and ultimately gave him a ride the rest of the way to the home of Jenny and Chris Lamey, who were packing up to move to a new home. Jenny Lamey was impressed with Carr and his story and they quickly developed a bond. In an article in the *Pelham Reporter*, Lamey said:

> "I just can't tell you how touched I was by Walter and his journey," she said. "He is humble and kind and cheerful, and he had big dreams! He is hardworking and tough. I can't imagine how many times on that lonely walk down 280 in the middle of the night did he want to turn back. How many times did he wonder if this was the best idea? How many times did he want to find a place to sit or lie down and wait 'til morning when he could maybe get someone to come pick him up and bring him back home? But he walked until he got here! I am in total awe of this young man!"

The next day, she posted about the experience on Facebook. Luke Marklin, CEO of Bellhops Movers, was so blown away by Carr's efforts he drove his own 2014 Ford Escort from Tennessee to personally give to Walter.

Carr wasn't prepared for the outpouring of support and media attention and was moved to tears by the gift of the car given to him by Marklin.

Since then, he has been featured on CNN, Fox News, NBC's Today Show, the BBC, and more. He's received multiple job offers and scholarship offers. Before he even had a Twitter account, he was the subject of tweets from Gov. Kay Ivey as well as US Ambassador to the UN, Nikki Haley.

There has even been a GoFundMe account set up for him by Jenny Lamey. It has always been Carr's goal to help people. He has decided to use his blessings to be a blessing to others (a long-time motto of the Birmingham City Schools graduate). He pledged, when the account was just over $65,000 that any additional money received from the GoFundMe account would go to the Birmingham Ed Foundation. (The Foundation is a non-profit dedicated to increasing the number of students in Birmingham City Schools who are on the path to college, career, and life-readiness.) The GoFundMe account now stands at over $90,000.

Walter Carr merely sought to be reliable and keep his commitment to his new employer. He is a humble young man who was looking for nothing more than making it to the job site and doing his work. His story has touched the hearts of thousands of people and in the process, he has received a windfall. So if you want to succeed in life—be like Walter. Be reliable!

Now, Munger does not only speak on the importance of reliability. In his address at the University of Southern California, he said, "the acquisition of wisdom is a moral duty."

I frequently tell the apocryphal story about how Max Planck, after he won the Nobel Prize, went around Germany giving the same standard lecture on the new quantum mechanics. Over time, his chauffeur memorized the lecture and said, "Would you mind, Professor Planck, because it's so boring to stay in routine, if I gave the lecture in Munich and you just sat in front wearing my chauffeur's hat? Planck said, "Why not?" And the chauffeur got up and gave this long lecture on quantum mechanics. After which a physics professor stood up and asked a perfectly ghastly question. The speaker said, "Well, I'm surprised that in an advanced city like Munich I get such an elementary question. I am going to ask my chauffeur to reply."

He shares this story to point out there are two types of knowledge. One is Planck knowledge, or what you would call real knowledge. These are people who have paid their dues and have real aptitude.

Too many modern people, he says, have chauffeur knowledge. That is more simple-minded knowledge. They try to appear to be knowledgeable to impress. He then gets a laugh when he tells these graduates that most of our politicians have chauffeur knowledge masquerading as real knowledge.

Munger believed that if we are to truly succeed in life, we have to discover within ourselves the discipline and the will to develop knowledge and understanding in the strategic areas of life.

We are clearly meant to be productive, and therefore, we should not just sell our businesses or retire and go to leisure world. Instead, we should find new work that adds meaning and purpose to our life.

4.8

The Formula
for Success

IN THE WORLD of business, one of the most frequent questions people ask is, "What is the one factor that contributes most to having a successful career?" I am sure if you asked all the experts in the top business schools you would in all likelihood get a multitude of answers. However, I have recently stumbled upon an insight that is worth considering.

Several years ago there was an article in *The Wall Street Journal* exploring the reasons executives fail. One of the top reasons given was a person's inability to effectively relate to others.

In their wonderful book, *When Smart People Fail*, authors Carole Hyatt and Linda Gottlieb made this interesting observation:

> Most careers involve other people. You can have great academic intelligence and still lack social intelligence—the ability to be a good listener, to be sensitive toward others, to give and take criticism well.
>
> If people don't like you, they may help you fail…On the other hand, you can get away with serious mistakes if you are socially intelligent …A mistake may actually further [your] career if the boss thinks [you] handled the situation in a mature and responsible way.

The Carnegie Foundation for the Advancement of Teaching discovered a significant fact in their research. In a person's career, 15% of one's financial success is due to one's technical knowledge and the other 85% is due to skills in human interaction and the ability to lead others.

Probably the most popular book ever written on human relations and human interaction is Dale Carnegie's *How To Win Friends And Influence People*. It has sold millions of copies and remains today a very popular book. In the book, Carnegie says:

> For many years, I conducted courses each season at the Engineers' Club of Philadelphia, and also courses for the New York Chapter of the American Institute Of Electrical Engineers. A total of probably more than fifteen hundred engineers have passed through my classes. They came to me because they had finally realized, after years of observation and experience, that the highest-paid personnel in engineering are frequently not those who know the most about engineering. One can for example, hire mere technical ability in engineering, accountancy, architecture or any other profession at nominal salaries. But the person who has technical knowledge plus the ability to express ideas, to assume leadership, and to arouse enthusiasm among people—that person is headed for higher earning power.

John D. Rockefeller is widely considered the wealthiest American of all time; the richest person in modern history. He founded the Standard Oil Company in 1870, which later became Exxon. Rockefeller recognized the significance of having good people skills. He said, "The ability to deal with people is as purchasable as a commodity of sugar or coffee. And I will pay more for that ability than for any other under the sun." Essentially, people skills make you stand out, above and beyond natural talent or delivered results.

Robert Rubin was a top executive at Goldman Sachs and former Secretary of the Treasury during the Clinton Administration. I recently was reading about Rubin and an event that completely transformed his life.

He reveals that in his early years at Goldman Sachs, he was, essentially, a jerk. He admits he was "short with people," "impersonal," "abrupt and peremptory," and frequently unkind to colleagues. None of this hindered his career as a successful arbitrageur: no one much cared how traders behaved as long as they delivered results. Then, one day, an older partner told Rubin he could possibly play a larger role in the firm if he changed his ways and actually started to care about the people he worked with.

As Rubin recalls in his memoir, "I've often asked myself why this advice affected me so much." He speculates on reasons, but the bottom line is that it affected him deeply. He started listening to people better, understanding their problems, and valuing their views. He changed an important element of his personality. If he hadn't, it's unlikely he would have become one of the most respected and admired figures at Goldman Sachs and on Wall Street.

Do you have social intelligence? Think about how you interact with people and how well you work with them. Are you a good listener or do you talk too much? Do you encourage others? Do you take an interest in their lives? Are you humble or are you always seeking to exalt yourself? Are you reliable and do you always do what you say you are going to do? Are you a team player?

I think author John Maxwell said it best:

> If you haven't learned how to get along with people, you will always be fighting a battle to succeed. However, making people skills a strength will take you farther than any other skill you develop. People like to do business with people they like. Or to put it the way President Theodore Roosevelt did: "The most important single ingredient in the formula of success is knowing how to get along with people."

5

Wisdom for Relationships

5.1

Protecting Our Greatest Treasure

A NUMBER of years ago, I read a very good book titled *Culture Shift* by David Henderson. In the book, he asks some very penetrating questions:

"Have you ever noticed there is a pattern when we buy something new? It can be a new television, a pair of hiking boots, a new car (anything)—it doesn't matter. It always happens. When we first get whatever it is, there is an energy we have, an excitement. It wakes us up and makes us alive.

But then, after a while—usually a pretty short while —there is a kind of sleepy dissatisfaction that comes over us. The new thing doesn't bring that energy anymore. It becomes familiar, normal, ordinary, and soon it blends in with everything else we own. Now we are restless for something else.

Have you ever stopped to think about what is going on here? There is something in us that yearns for something outside of us that will settle our hearts, that will give us peace, satisfaction, fulfillment."

What we all must realize is that all material objects decrease in enjoyment and satisfaction over time. This is because our possessions fail to give us any degree of lasting happiness. This is a part of the fabric of life.

This reminds me of the words of the great French historian, Alexis de Tocqueville, who toured America back in the 1830s and wrote the well-known book *Democracy in America.* He noticed "a strange melancholy that haunts the inhabitants . . . in the midst of abundance." He saw that Americans had come to believe that prosperity and material wealth could quench their yearning for happiness. His response: "the incomplete joys of this world will never satisfy the human heart."

I think we sometimes miss a vital truth. There is only one thing in this life that can grow in love and enjoyment over time and bring genuine happiness into our lives, and that, of course, is our relationships.

Alexandr Solzhenitsyn said, "It is not the level of prosperity that makes for a high quality of life—but it is the kinship of one person's heart to another's heart."

The great thing about relationships is that they are organic. They have the capacity to grow in love, intimacy, depth, and enjoyment over time. However, they have to be properly nurtured and cared for.

Relationships are the essence of life. They are the foundation of happiness.

However, if this is true, we should be doing everything in our power to develop, protect, and nurture all these relationships. Yet, I am amazed that the priorities in the lives of so many people are not focused here, and they wonder why life is so disappointing.

Jerry Leachman tells a great story of a meeting he had with a very powerful, wealthy man in Washington D.C. A mutual friend had arranged the meeting in hopes that Jerry might help this man whose family life was in shambles. After talking for an hour or so Jerry made this observation: "From what you have told me, it does not sound to me like your family is much of a priority in your life."

With that, the man stood up as if he wanted to fight Jerry. He said in an angry loud voice, "How dare you accuse me of not loving my family."

Jerry responded calmly, "I did not say you didn't love them, I said they were not a priority to you. From what you have told me, your business is your first priority." It was like a ton of bricks had fallen on this man. It finally dawned on him what he had done to his family. The next day he decided to sell his business.

As you examine your own life, ask yourself, what is your greatest treasure and what are you doing to protect it?

5.2

Thoughts on Friendship

I ONCE HAD a friend send me a hilarious sketch from an episode of "Saturday Night Live." The sketch refers to studies concluding that males in America are increasingly friendless. In the sketch, a young woman, frustrated by her boyfriend's inability to open up to anyone else, takes him by the hand and leads him to a "man park" (like the dog version). After a shy start, he finds fellow males to make friends with. Now some viewers may have disliked the likening of men to dogs, but I believe the sketch, which went viral online, illustrated fresh concerns about an old worry: the loneliness of American men.

I was reminded of an incident in the life of author and speaker Gordon MacDonald. He spent a day addressing a group of 50 nuclear scientists. These were all men who had multiple PhD degrees from MIT. They had been involved in projects revolving around nuclear submarines and now were consulting with nuclear power plants around the world. In the first hour of his presentation, he made the comment that mid-life men are terribly lonely. One of the men in the audience raised his hand and asked, "Mr. MacDonald, can you tell us why we are lonely?" Mr. MacDonald made a few comments on the need for intimacy and friendship. Then, another man raised his hand and asked, "Can you tell us how to make a friend?" MacDonald thought to himself, "I am being asked one of the most simple questions in life by some of the most brilliant people in the land; Men who have had their fingers on nuclear missiles the past 10 years." For the next 2 hours, MacDonald said they were totally captivated as he spoke on how to find intimacy. They each acknowledged they were terribly lonely.

When I am asked why the Center for Executive Leadership works predominantly with men, I explain quite simply, "Because women are much healthier than men. They are more transparent than men, and they have deeper friendships. They are not afraid to share their struggles with one another."

That is not to say that women do not have their own issues with friendship. Many of the women in my life have made comments about how while female friendships are often more transparent, they are also much more nuanced in the ways they deal with conflict, jealousy, and constant comparison. However, on the topic of emotional availability, men are simply a different animal.

Perhaps part of this has to do with the way that men are traditionally raised in comparison to women. Young girls are often taught to be open, nurturing, and feel deeply. They are given baby dolls and are told they are made of "sugar and spice and everything nice." Boys, however, are supposed to be tough. They are given little trucks and toy soldiers and are often told to "toughen up" and "be a man," even when emotion is extremely warranted. Of course, this is not the case for all children, but it has certainly been the cultural norm for a long time. To think that this does not have at least some impact on the way we grow into adulthood and interact with others would be foolish.

Joe Ehrmann says the true mark of a man, and I would argue people in general, is found in the quality of his relationships —the capacity one has to love and be loved. When we reach the end of our lives and look back, the only thing that is really going to matter is the quality of the relationships we've had.

There are so many important relationships in life. We could talk about marriage or our relationships with our children, but here are a couple of observations about friendships. I believe this is such an important issue because friendships and quality relationships are so hard to come by, yet friendship can bring something into our lives that marriage and family cannot.

Ehrmann laments the fact that men are always comparing and competing, wondering how they measure up to other men. It leaves them with feelings of isolation and loneliness. Now, this is not exclusive to men as women, too, are constantly comparing themselves to one another, but as a man in his seventies, I can not quite speak to that experience. Although, I would imagine the emotional impacts are quite similar. However, the major difference here lies in a study that Coach Ehrmann mentions which reveals a sad fact: most men over the age of thirty-five have no authentic friends—someone close to them with whom they can be vulnerable and share their innermost thoughts and feelings.

Armond Nicholi, Jr., in his book, *The Question of God*, tells about C. S. Lewis's view of friendship. Lewis, for years an atheist, had a very pessimistic view of life and had no friends. As a Christian, his view of life and relationships was transformed. As Nicholi put it, nothing brought Lewis more enjoyment than sitting around a fire with a group of close friends engaged in good discussion or talking long walks through the English countryside.

"My happiest hours," Lewis wrote, "are spent with three or four old friends in old clothes tramping together and putting up in small pub—or else sitting up 'til the small hours in someone's college rooms, talking nonsense, poetry, theology, metaphysics.... There's no sound I like better than ... laughter."

In another letter to his good friend, Greeves, Lewis writes, "Friendship is the greatest of worldly goods. Certainly to me it is the chief happiness of life. If I had to give a piece of advice to a young man about a place to live, I think I should say, 'sacrifice almost everything you have to live where you can be near your friends.' Lewis changed from a wary introvert with very few close relationships to a personable extrovert with scores of close friends and colleagues. George Sayer, a biographer who knew Lewis for some thirty years, and Owen Barfield, a close friend for over forty years, described Lewis after his conversion, "He was unusually cheerful, and took an almost boyish delight" in life. [They] describe him as "great fun, an extremely witty and amusing companion . . . considerate . . . more concerned with the welfare of his friends than with himself."

I think Lewis recognized that without great friendships, life is virtually bankrupt. Furthermore, it strikes me that really good friendships have to be deliberately pursued and forged over time. The building of a good friendship requires effort. And when we are willing to come out of hiding, be vulnerable, and be willing to share our secrets with a close friend or two, these friendships deepen. It seems that the power to honor the truth and speak the truth openly is at the heart of a healthy, authentic person.

5.3

The Power
of Transparency

OVER THE YEARS, I have noticed one of the great struggles we have is how we compare ourselves with others. We may or may not be aware of this struggle, but we would never want anyone to know about it, particularly the feelings of inferiority we might experience from the comparison.

Dennis Prager shares a very enlightening illustration of how this might play out in our lives:

Two couples leave their homes to meet for dinner at a restaurant. Couple A has a big fight on the way to dinner, as does Couple B. But when the two couples finally arrive at the restaurant, they all act as if everything is fine.

"Hi, how are you two doing?" they both ask one another.

"Fine, great. And how are you two? They both reply.

During dinner, neither couple utters a word about their fight. Driving home, couple A says to each other, "Did you see couple B—how happy and in love they are? Why can't we be that happy?" Meanwhile, in their car, couple B are saying the exact same thing: "Did you see couple A— how happy and in love they are? Why can't we be that happy?"

Not only were the couples unhappy from their respective fights, but they are now even more unhappy as a result of comparing themselves with the other couple! They suffer from what can be called compound unhappiness—just as compound interest is interest on interest, compound unhappiness is unhappiness over being unhappy. Such are the dangers of comparing ourselves with others.

The unhappiness of these two couples was unnecessarily compounded by comparing themselves with the other couple, but even their original unhappiness over their fighting could have been reduced. How?

Had the two couples not put on a happy act and opened up to one another, each couple would have left the restaurant happier than when they entered it. All one couple had to do was respond to "How are you guys doing?" with something like, "We're all right, but boy, did we have a fight right before coming here tonight." The odds are overwhelming that if these couples were at all close, the other couple would have responded, "You did? We did too!"

Then, instead of acting as if nothing had happened and everything was wonderful, the couples would be free, thanks to one couple telling the truth, to talk about their respective fights. And if the fights were within the normal range of marital arguments, opening up and finding out that virtually every couple has fights, often about the same things, would have brought everyone closer together. In fact, much marital grief would be avoided if married people talked about their marriages to other married people. In most cases, learning that virtually every marriage has its share of problems, many of which are universal, and then talking—even joking—about them leads to a genuine reduction in marital stress.

I think this illustration reveals two important truths. First, we should recognize that in all areas of life, our joy and happiness would increase if we stopped comparing ourselves with other people. Particularly those whom we always imagine to be happier than us. Remember, everyone in life is fighting a battle of some kind, no one's life is trouble-free.

Second, I would remind you of the power of being transparent with others. We all have this natural tendency to hide ourselves from others and we do this by wearing certain masks. Bill Thrall, in his book *TrueFaced*, states eventually all our masks will crack, and inevitably, our true selves will be exposed.

Thrall, however, offers us an interesting, deeper view of life's difficulties. He suggests that the struggles we face could be the best things that could ever happen to us. If our masks succeed and help us to remain hidden and protected, who would ever really know us? We would be totally inauthentic, living only to perform for and impress others. Most significantly, we might go through all our days missing out on the life God intended for us.

5.4

The Difference a Family Makes

MUCH HAS been written recently about the nuclear family. There are many who are questioning whether it is necessary to have a strong family. Does it really make a difference?

In the *Forbes Book of Business Quotations,* Perry F. Webb says this about the family:

> "The home . . . is the lens through which we get our first look at marriage and all civic duties; it is the clinic where, by conversation and Attitude, impressions are created with respect to sobriety and reverence; it is the school where lessons of truth or falsehood, honesty or deceit are learned; it is the mold which ultimately determines the structure of society."

I recently read a research study done by Richard L. Dugdale back in 1874.

As a member of the executive committee of the Prison Association of New York, he was chosen to inspect thirteen county jails in the state. When he got to one particular county, he was surprised to discover that six people related by blood were in the same jail. They were being held on a variety of offenses including burglary, attempted rape, and assault with intent to kill. When Dugdale talked to the county sheriff and an eighty-four-year-old physician, he discovered that the family had been in the area since the settling of New York State and they were notorious for their criminal behavior.

Dugdale was intrigued, and he decided to study the family and publish what he found, using the fictitious name "Jukes" to describe them. He traced their line back to a man he called Max, born sometime between 1720 and 1740. He had six daughters and two sons. Some of his children were born out of wedlock. He was a heavy drinker and wasn't known to be particularly fond of work.

Dugdale estimated the family probably comprised about 1,200 people, but he was able to study only 709 members of the family. In 1877, he published his findings in *The Jukes: A Study in Crime, Pauperism, Disease, and Heredity*. He found they exhibited a pattern of criminality, harlotry, and pauperism that defied statistical averages:

- 180 were paupers (25 percent)
- 140 were criminals (20 percent)
- 60 were habitual thieves (8.5 percent)
- 50 were common sex workers (7 percent)

The family's reputation was so bad, according to Dugdale, "Their family name had come to be used generically as a term of reproach." The owner of a factory in the area used to keep a list of Jukes family members' names in his office to make sure none of them got hired.

Dugdale and many subsequent researchers desired to establish the role heredity played in the behavior of the Jukes family. Today, scientists agree that there is no "criminal" gene to explain behavior. Clearly, there were members of the Jukes family who escaped the cycle of crime and self-destruction. But one thing is certain: Being in the Jukes family had a negative, destabilizing effect on the lives of many people.

Ironically, at about the same time and in the same general region, there was another family that had a significantly different kind of pattern.

The family is that of Jonathan Edwards, the theologian, pastor, and president of Princeton, who was born in 1703 and lived in Connecticut, New York, Massachusetts, and New Jersey. Edwards was a devoted family man. He and his wife, Sarah, had eleven children—three sons and eight daughters. They remained married for 31 years until he died of fever following a smallpox inoculation.

In 1900, A.E. Winship studied 1,400 descendants of Jonathan and Sarah Edwards. Among them, Winship found:

- 13 college presidents
- 65 professors
- 100 lawyers, including a law school dean
- 30 judges
- 66 physicians, including a medical school dean
- 80 holders of public office, including 3 U.S. senators, 3 mayors of large cities, 3 governors, a controller of the U.S. Treasury, and a U.S. vice president

I feel certain that not all of Edward's descendants were high achievers. However, I do believe that having a stable, loving family can give an individual a real advantage in life.

Of course, not all families look the same, but that doesn't matter. At the end of the day, it is about having a family of loved ones who are there to teach, support, and encourage you to be the best version of yourself.

If you are raising your own family, I would remind you of the words of John Maxwell: "While you can't do much about your ancestors, you can influence your descendants greatly."

5.5

Love and Marriage

STEPHEN COVEY was speaking at a conference on being pro-active in your marriage, and when he was finished, he was approached by a man who said to him:

"Stephen, I like what you're saying. But every situation is so different. Look at my marriage. I'm really worried. My wife and I just don't have the same feelings for each other we used to have. I guess I just don't love her anymore and she doesn't love me. What can I do?"

"The feeling isn't there anymore?" I asked.

"That's right," he reaffirmed. "And we have three children we're really concerned about. What do you suggest?"

"Love her," I replied.

"I told you, the feeling just isn't there anymore."

"Love her."

"You don't understand. The feeling of love just isn't there."

"Then love her. If the feeling isn't there, that's a good reason to love her."

"But how do you love when you don't love?"

"My friend, love is a verb. Love—the feeling—is a

fruit of love, the verb. So love her. Serve her. Sacrifice. Listen to her. Empathize. Appreciate. Affirm her. Are you willing to do that?"

Modern people seem to be driven by their feelings, and no doubt Hollywood has had something to do with that, particularly when it comes to our feelings about romantic love. It is as if we can abdicate our responsibilities in our romantic relationships the second we lose feelings.

Love is something you do, particularly the sacrifices you are willing to make for the one you love. I remember many years ago hearing an obstetrician speak. He said mothers are so devoted and have such a deep love for their children because of the incredible sacrifices they have made in bringing their children into the world and then nurturing them through childhood. His point was that the more you sacrifice for someone, the greater the love you will have for them.

Dr. Tim Keller says:

> Nearly everyone thinks that the Bible's directive to "love your neighbor" is wise, right and good. But, notice that it is a command, and emotions cannot be commanded. The Bible does not call us to like our neighbor, to have affection and warm feelings toward him or her. No, the call is to love your neighbor, and that must primarily mean displaying a set of behaviors.

We know feelings are real, but they are not reliable. Feelings are not consistent and are tied to a number of complex factors, waxing and waning. Dr. Keller makes a solid point: our emotions are not always under our control, but our actions are.

I know of a counselor who strongly believes that feelings of love will follow acts of love. When he counsels those who are struggling in their marriage, he lays out a challenge for them, asking for a four-week commitment. Every day for the next four weeks, they are to do five things each day that someone in love would do. Each morning, they are to make a list of five specific things to do for the other person to express love.

The results? Invariably, over that four-week period, couples begin to see real progress. Unfortunately, most spouses refuse to accept this challenge because they do not think that they are responsible for their marital problems. In reality, they are too lazy to put forth the effort to love their spouse, seeing divorce as an easier alternative.

The same applies to long-term relationships, whether you have yet to be married or not. Especially for my younger readers, one of the biggest markers of a strong relationship is whether or not you are willing to go on loving through your actions instead of running away the second the original spark begins to fade.

Author C.S. Lewis strongly believed that even if you have feelings of indifference toward the one you love, you can change your heart over the long haul through your actions. Now is the perfect time to ask yourself—am I truly loving through my actions?

5.6

Thoughts on Relational Conflict

IN ANY romantic relationship, but especially in a marriage, conflict can manifest itself on various levels of complexity. Some conflicts are singular and can be resolved easily, while others become lost within a black hole, leading to breakups and divorce.

I have two concepts to consider when addressing marital conflict, with my first thought reflected in a post by Dr. Tim Keller:

> When I was a young pastor in a small Southern town, I did a lot of marriage counseling. Some marriages were harmed by things like drink, drugs, pornography or an extramarital affair. But, in most of the troubled marriages I saw, the problem stemmed not from bad things but from very good things that had become too important. When some good thing becomes more engrossing and important than your spouse, it can destroy the marriage.

He goes on to mention that if your spouse does not feel you are putting him or her first, then by definition, you are not. When this happens, your marriage or relationship is dying.

According to Dr. Keller, there are four primary "good things" we overcommit to in marital conflict.

The first and most obvious is our children. A strong marriage between husband and wife makes children grow up feeling the world is a safe place and love is possible. It is healthy for children to see that the marriage comes first.

On the other hand, take a look at a mother who puts her children above her husband. It not only harms the marriage, but the children do not get to see how a good marriage works. By putting her children before her husband, she does not realize she is harming the children.

The second good thing is our parents. Some people never leave their parents. We are told to "Leave our fathers and mothers and cleave to our spouse." Often, people don't leave their parents and allow them to become too involved in their lives.

The third good thing is work. This is highly common in this age where people are driven to be successful. If either person perceives that work is their top priority and more important than spending time with the one they love, the relationship will slowly die.

The final good thing is our hobbies. If one person truly devotes more time, effort, and attention to a hobby than to their marriage or relationship, the relationship is really in trouble.

My second thought on romantic conflict has to do with blame. When a relationship is in trouble, especially in marriage, it is easy to point the finger at each other. They generally acknowledge they are partly to blame, but the real problem is the other person.

I believe Jesus gives thoughtful insight regarding this issue in the Sermon on the Mount:

> And why do you look at the speck that is in your brother's eye, but do not notice the log that is in your own eye? Or how can you say to your 'Let me take the speck out of your eye,' and behold, the log is in your own eye? You hypocrite, first take the log out of your own eye, and then you will see clearly to take the speck out of your brother's eye." (Mathew 7:3-5)

Here, Jesus tells us we have a propensity to easily point out the flaws in the lives of others when we are so blind to the major shortcomings in our own lives. This is particularly true in marriage.

Best-selling author Henry Cloud writes about this in his book *Boundaries in Marriage*. He recalls a therapy session with Caroline and Joe, a couple who sought counseling because they couldn't stop arguing.

When prompted to explain why they argued so much, Caroline said it was because Joe was angry all the time, gets mad at her, and is so mean.

Dr. Cloud responded by swinging his head over to Joe. "Why do you get so mad?" he asked.

"Because she always tries to control me and my life," Joe responded immediately.

Dr. Cloud then whooshed his head towards Caroline, sensing he was about to witness "a game of Ping-Pong."

"Why do you try to control him?" he asked Caroline.

"Because he is so into his own things that I can't get his time or attention," she replied.

On and on it went. Back and forth. Back and forth.

Neither took ownership of their actions or reactions. It was always because of the other person.

Dr. Cloud "longed for Joe to say, for example, 'I get angry at her because I'm too immature to respond to her more helpfully. I'm deeply sorry for that and need some help. I want to be able to love her correctly no matter what her behavior is. Can you help me?'"

Does this sound familiar? One phrase is at the heart of most relational conflicts: *It is not my fault.* This is why Dr. Cloud believes that blame is the essence of character flaws.

Author Gary Thomas has this to add:

"I have a theory, behind virtually every case of marital dissatisfaction lies an unwillingness to admit our self-centeredness. Couples do not fall out of love so much as they are unwilling to humbly acknowledge they have short-comings as a spouse. Flaws and personal failures that are not dealt with slowly erode the relationship, assaulting and, eventually, erasing the once lofty promise in the throes of an earlier and less polluted love."

What do you think would happen if two people who recognized their marriage was deteriorating and moving toward divorce were both willing to humble themselves and say, "This is on me. I am the problem, I am at fault. I will no longer point the finger at my spouse. I am going to focus on my shortcomings and where I have failed in this marriage."

What do you think might possibly happen?

Someone recently shared with me the lyrics of a song performed by Vince Gill. The opening lyrics are, "Let there be peace on earth, and let it begin with me."

As we go through this life, we will always have conflicts in our relationships. As we seek peace and reconciliation, we must be willing to "let it begin with me."

6

Wisdom for
Character Issues

6.1

Living for Appearances

OVER THE YEARS, in all of my teaching, speaking, and writing, the most popular illustration I have ever used is clearly Gordon MacDonald's "The Wreck of *the Persona*." In fact, I used it in the opening chapter of my book, *The True Measure of a Man*.

Once, a very prosperous man decided to build for himself a sailing yacht. His intention was that it would be the most talked-about boat that ever sailed. He was determined to spare no expense or effort.

As he built his craft, the man outfitted it with colorful sails, complex rigging, and comfortable conveniences in the cabin. The decks were made from teakwood; all the fittings were custom-made of polished brass. And on the stern, painted in gold letter, readable from a considerable distance, was the name of the boat, *The Persona*.

As he built *The Persona*, the man could not resist fantasizing upon the anticipated admiration and applause from club members at the launching of his new boat. In fact, the more he thought about the praise that was soon to come, the more time and attention he gave to the boat's appearance.

Now—and this seems reasonable—because no one would ever see the underside of *The Persona*, the man saw little need to be concerned about the keel, or, for that matter, anything that had to do with the issues of properly distributed weight and ballast.

The boat builder was acting with the perceptions of the crowd in his mind—not the seaworthiness of the vessel. Seaworthiness seems not to be an important issue when one is on a dry dock.

"Why should I spend money or time on what is out of sight? When I listen to the conversations of people at the club, I hear them praising only what they can see," he told himself. "I never remember anyone admiring the underside of a boat. Instead, I sense that my yachting colleagues really find exciting the color and shape of a boat's sails, its brass fittings, its cabin and creature comforts, decks and wood texture, potential speed, and the skill that wins the Sunday afternoon regattas."

And so, driven by such reasoning, the man built his boat. Everything that would be visible to the people soon began to gleam with excellence. But things that would be invisible when the boat entered the water were generally ignored. People did not seem to take notice of this, or if they did, they made no comment.

The builder's sorting out priorities of resources and time proved to be correct: members of the boat club did indeed understand and appreciate the sails, rigging, decks, brass, and staterooms. And what they saw, they praised. On occasion, he overheard some say that his efforts to build the grandest boat in the history of the club would certainly result in his selection as commodore.

When the day came for the maiden voyage, the people of the club joined him dockside. A bottle of champagne was broken over the bow, and the moment came for the man to set sail. As the breeze filled the sails and pushed *The Persona* from the club's harbor, he stood at the helm and heard what he'd anticipated for years: the cheers and well-wishes of envious admirers who said to one another, "Our club has never seen a grander boat than this. This man will make us the talk of the yachting world."

Soon, *The Persona* was merely a blip on the horizon. As it cut through the swells, its builder and owner gripped the rudder with a feeling of fierce pride. What he had accomplished! He was seized with an increasing rush of confidence that everything —the boat, his future as a boat club member (and probably as commodore), and even the ocean—was his to control.

But a few miles out to see, a storm arose. Not a hurricane —but not a squall either. There were sudden gusts in excess of forty knots and waves above fifteen feet. *The Persona* began to shudder, and water swept over the sides. Bad things began to happen, and the poise of the captain began to waiver. Perhaps the ocean wasn't his after all.

Within minutes, *The Persona's* colorful sails were in shreds, the splendid mast was splintered in pieces, and the rigging was unceremoniously draped all over the bow. The teakwood decks and the lavishly appointed cabin were awash with water. And then, before the man could prepare himself, a wave bigger than anything he'd ever seen hurled down upon *The Persona*, and the boat capsized.

Now, this is important—most boats would have righted themselves after such a battering. *The Persona* did not. Why? Because its builder had ignored the importance of what was below the waterline. There was no weight there. In a moment when a well-designed keel and adequate ballast might have saved the ship, they were nowhere to be found. The man had concerned himself with the appearance of things and not enough with the needed resilience and stability in the secret, unseen places where storms are withstood.

Furthermore, because the foolish man had such confidence in his sailing abilities, he had never contemplated the possibility of a situation he could not manage. And that's why later investigations revealed that there were no rescue devices aboard: no rafts, life jackets, or emergency radios. The result of this mixture of poor planning and blind pride was the foolish man was lost at sea.

Only when the wreckage of *The Persona* was washed ashore did the man's boat club friends discover all of this. They said, "Only a fool would design and build a boat like this, much less sail in it. A man who builds only above the waterline does not realize that he has built less than half a boat. Didn't he understand that a boat not built with storms in mind is a floating disaster waiting to happen? How absurd that we should have applauded him so enthusiastically." The foolish man was never found. Today, when people speak of him—which is rare—they comment not upon the initial success of the man or upon the beauty of his boat, but only upon the silliness of putting it out on an ocean where storms are sudden and violent. Even more, doing it with a boat that was really never built for anything else but the vanity of its builder and the praise of spectators. It was in such conversations that the owner of *The Persona*, whose name has long been forgotten, became known as simply the foolish man.

I find that when I share this story with people it speaks powerfully into their lives. It is one of the clearest examples of how we can develop such a misguided understanding of how to measure our lives. Furthermore, if we do not have a solid foundation of character and wisdom which we have built our lives upon, we will crash and burn when the storms blow into our lives.

6.2

A Life
Without Constraints

THE GREAT political philosopher Edmund Burke made this insightful observation over 200 years ago: "Freedom without wisdom or responsibility is the greatest of all possible evils." This is a very sobering statement, yet I wonder if modern people recognize the truthfulness of these words.

I have concluded that many Americans believe freedom means the absence of restraints in our lives. As long as we can follow our hearts and as long as we do not hurt anyone, the absence of restraints is the key to a full and happy life—to fulfill all of our yearnings and desires.

If you look around the world today, this modern view of freedom is clearly not working. It does not lead to happiness, and it never will, because this way of thinking inevitably breaks down, leading to chaos and pain. In fact, I would say this model of freedom explains why people's lives are not working in a progressive culture that seems to have it all.

I was recently reading Jonathan Haidt's popular book, *The Happiness Hypothesis*. Haidt is a professor of psychology at the University of Virginia and seems to have good insight into the human condition.

In the book, he speaks of Émile Durkheim, one of the founders of sociology in the late nineteenth century. Durkheim performed a massive scholarly study, gathering data from all across

Europe, and studying the factors that affect the suicide rate. All of his findings can be summarized in one word; "constraints."

He discovered that no matter how he parsed the data, people who had fewer social constraints and obligations were more likely to kill themselves. Durkheim concluded from all of his research that people need obligations and constraints to provide structure and meaning to their lives. This is what provides order and keeps out chaos.

One of the examples Durkheim gives relates to our social lives. He points out that one of the greatest obligations in life is found in marriage. In one sense, when you marry you are giving up your freedom and bringing all kinds of constraints into your life.

Durkheim's research showed that people living alone were most likely to take their own lives, married people less, and married people with children even less.

Today, marriage rates are in rapid decline because so many people do not want to be tied down and give up their freedom. In 2019, I read that the current marriage rate was the lowest it has been in 150 years. Durkheim concludes an ideology of extreme personal freedom can be dangerous because it encourages people to leave homes, jobs, cities, and marriages in search of personal and professional fulfillment, thereby breaking the relationships that were probably their best hope for such fulfillment.

Pastor Tim Keller says sometimes you have to deliberately give up your freedom to engage in activities and thought processes that will enable you to release yourself to a richer kind of freedom. And as we look at the competing desires of our hearts, we must discover which of our desires are liberating and which are destructive. Ultimately, we need to determine which of our desires are aligned with who we really are, and therefore, enhance our lives, and not destroy them.

In our quest for happiness, we must recognize that freedom is not a lack of restrictions; rather, it is finding the right restrictions. Freedom occurs when you discover the restrictions that are best for your being and lead to harmony, peace, and joy in your life.

6.3

The Dragon in the Room

CLOSE TO twenty-five years ago, I read some words from Jack Welch that had a real impact on my life. Welch took General Electric, a faltering home appliance company, and transformed it into one of the most successful conglomerates in the world. He retired in 2001, and since then, the company has declined dramatically.

Welch became GE's youngest CEO in 1982. As he sought to transform the company, he embraced a certain guiding principle that drove everything. These words really resonated with me:

> "The key trait of a vital, dynamic corporation is looking reality (the truth) straight in the eye, and then acting on it with as much speed as possible."

Welch says that when he became CEO, he inherited a lot of great things, but facing the truth, particularly as it relates to problems, was not one of the company's strengths. They had too much superficial congeniality and unrealistic optimism. This made candor extremely difficult to come by.

What I learned from Welch is that if you want to be a healthy person or a healthy organization, you have to run toward your problems and not away from them.

You see this same teaching in Jordan Peterson's *The 12 Rules for Life*. He says if you want real chaos in your life, don't deal with your problems. Let them linger, ignore them, pretend like they are not there.

I think we somehow come to believe that maybe if we don't deal with them, they will eventually go away. However, they never go away. In fact, most problems that are not confronted grow worse over time, becoming magnified and compounded.

Peterson is a brilliant psychologist who teaches at the University of Toronto. To make his point, he uses a simple children's story to teach this valuable lesson.

> It comes from the book, *There's No Such Thing as a Dragon*, by Jack Kent. It's a very simple tale, at least on the surface. It's about a small boy, Billy Bixbee, who spies a dragon sitting on his bed one morning. It's about the size of a house cat, and friendly. He tells his mother about it, but she tells him there's no such thing as a dragon. So, it starts to grow. It eats all of Billy's pancakes. Soon it fills the whole house. Mom tries to vacuum, but she has to go in and out of the house through the windows because of the dragon everywhere. It takes her forever. Then, the dragon runs off with the house. Billy's dad comes home – and there's just an empty space, where he used to live. The mailman tells him where the house went. He chases after it, climbs up the dragon's head and neck (now sprawling out into the street) and rejoins his wife and son. Mom still insists that the dragon does not exist, but Billy, who's pretty much had it by now, insists, "There is a dragon, Mom." Instantly, it starts to shrink. Soon, it's cat-sized again. Everyone agrees that dragons of that size (1) exist and (2) are much preferable to their giant counterparts. Mom, eyes reluctantly opened by this point, asks somewhat plaintively why it had to get so big. Billy quietly suggests: "Maybe it wanted to be noticed."

Peterson says we love to sweep our problems under the rug, however, this is where dragons feast on crumbs, resulting in rapid growth. Then one day, it bursts forth in a way that you can no longer ignore, and the result is usually chaos and misery.

This can happen within your family, company, friendships, or more severely, in your overall life. Peterson says it happens most frequently in marriage. When marital conflict and problems arise, so many couples don't react, don't discuss, don't attend to it, don't work for peace, and don't take responsibility. He says that the possibility of a growing dragon lurks beneath every marriage.

Therefore, if you want to be a healthy person and have healthy relationships, you must run straight at your problems and not away from them. The alternative is a chaotic life full of misery.

6.4

A Modern Parable

WHEN I wrote the book *The Power of a Humble Life,* I wanted to illustrate the different types of pride and how they manifest in our lives. It starts by comparing ourselves to others with the belief that we are superior to those we are comparing ourselves with. It is important to recognize that pride emanates from a multitude of sources: wealth, achievement, power, beauty, and knowledge.

However, there is a pride that many believe is the most dangerous. It is the pride of virtue, of believing you are morally superior to others. It is called self-righteousness. To better illustrate this, I wrote the following parable.

Steven and Samuel Chamberlain were identical twin brothers, born in 1965. They grew up in Memphis, Tennessee, and were inseparable. They both were serious students and great athletes. Steven was the quarterback on their high school football team, while Samuel was the team's star receiver. In the spring they both played baseball.

Though it was a difficult decision, they decided to attend different colleges. Steven enrolled at the University of North Carolina, and Samuel went to Wake Forest. The four years flew by and both young men flourished socially and academically. It was during their senior year that they both were notified they had been accepted into the Vanderbilt School of Medicine. It was a dream come true.

Medical school was difficult and the hours were long, but the two brothers excelled in their schoolwork and training. Steven Chamberlain became a well-known orthopedic surgeon and Samuel a very well-respected vascular surgeon. They both moved back to Memphis and began their medical practices. As the years went by they married, had children, and remained very close. Both of their families eventually moved to a very fine suburb called Mountain Ridge. The two families lived just down the street from each other. Life was good.

One day Steven received a call from one of his patients. This particular patient was a very distinguished realtor in their community, and he revealed to Steven, confidentially, that he had just been given the listing on a piece of the most coveted land in Mountain Ridge. It was one hundred acres of choice property on top of the small mountain for which the community was named.

Steven realized he could build his dream home on this property, and he would have an incredible view of the community below. It would be a showplace that everyone in Mountain Ridge could look up to and see. Within an hour, he had spoken to his wife and they made the offer at list price.

News that this choice piece of property had been sold spread quickly throughout the community. Everyone was curious to see the magnificent house that would be built on the hill.

It took over two years for the house to be constructed; once it was finished, it was captivating, particularly at night when it was all lit up.

It was an 8,000-square-foot house with seven bedrooms and ten bathrooms. It had an indoor and outdoor pool, tennis courts, and a stable for their daughter's horses. When the couple decided to have a big gala to allow people in the community to see their new home, everyone was anxious about whether they would be invited or not.

Every morning Steven woke up and walked out on one of his balconies with a cup of coffee and the Wall Street Journal in hand and looked down on the town below. Without realizing it, he gloated, knowing that he lived in the nicest home in Mountain Ridge and probably all of Memphis. He reasoned to himself that he had worked hard for it and therefore clearly deserved the beautiful place.

Also every morning, Samuel woke up down in the suburbs below. He too sipped on a cup of coffee on his modest backyard porch where he had a perfect view of his brother's beautiful home. He thought to himself, "That pompous, arrogant brother of mine. He is so full of himself." He thought about his own life and gloated over the fact that he had a much more modest lifestyle than his brother and could therefore give more money to the church and to charity. He also reflected on the fact that his children were not nearly as spoiled as his brother's, who were real brats. He was very proud of his wise choices and good works as he compared his life and family with those of his brother.

In this parable, you find both of these brothers are guilty of pride. The first brother, Steven, was comparing his possessions and material wealth to everyone else's in the community. It caused him to have a feeling of superiority over them.

He was guilty of buying something not primarily for its usefulness, but for the way it made him appear in the eyes of others. He did it to impress people, to proclaim to the world he was wealthy. Steven was guilty of pride, and it was quite obvious. The entire community could see it!

It is important to recognize that pride emanates from a multitude of sources: wealth, achievement, power, beauty, and knowledge. However, there is a pride that Reinhold Niebuhr believed is the most dangerous—the pride of virtue, or what is called self-righteousness. Self-righteousness is what Samuel is guilty of. It is important to notice how comparison is at work. He compares himself to his brother who lives up on the hill. He compares their lifestyles and concludes that he is morally superior, and naturally presumes that he is so much more righteous than his brother.

What I find to be so interesting is that through comparison, each of these men is guilty of pride. In Steven's case, it's not quite as hard for you to detect when you are trying to impress others, and it is certainly even more apparent to everyone else. Samuel's problem, self-righteousness, is much more difficult to detect within ourselves because we become blinded by our own perceived goodness. In Samuel's mind, all he could see was the good he was doing. "I am living modestly; I am giving money away; I am doing so much good for the community, unlike my extravagant, pompous brother."

Though both brothers were guilty of pride, neither of them could see it in their lives, and this is why C.S. Lewis says pride is "the chief cause of misery in every nation and every family since the beginning of time."

6.5

Forgiveness is for the Forgiver

RECENTLY, I READ the dramatic account of a young woman whose story was told on a BBC broadcast in 2013. Natascha Kampusch, a ten-year-old Austrian girl was abducted on the way to school by a man in his mid-thirties. He locked her in a dark, dungeon-like room underneath his garage, where he kept her for eight years. After a while, he would let her out to cook for him and do household chores, always under close guard, before locking her in the concrete room each night. At times, he beat her so badly she could hardly walk. He also raped her.

When Natascha finally escaped to a neighbor's house, as an eighteen-year-old, she weighed about the same (105 pounds) as when she entered. Despite the horrific ordeal, she came to a place of forgiveness. As she explained on the program, "I felt I had to forgive him. Only by doing so could I push it away from myself. If I hadn't been able to forgive him then these feelings of frustration and anger would have continued to eat away at me and would have lived on—this entire experience would have continued to live on inside me. It is as if he would have won in the end if I had let that get to me. I didn't want hate to poison me because hate always backfires, it comes back on yourself."

What tremendous wisdom and courage this young woman possessed. She recognized that if she was not able to forgive the perpetrator, he would have defeated her. She would be trapped in her anger for the rest of her life.

We do not seem to realize that we are what we remember. The past and what our mind does not let go of does not necessarily determine who we are, but it shapes our lives. Furthermore, if we do not recognize and deal with the baggage in our lives from the past, it can sabotage our lives now and in the future—particularly our relationships. So many people I encounter are not even aware of how their refusal or inability to reconcile with the past has messed up their lives. Many who are aware of it refuse to deal with it. The thought of having to deal with the past can be so frightening. It can paralyze us.

Anger, bitterness, and hatred are all linked together, and they are all about the past. Past hurts—in which people have wronged us, injured us, abused us, mocked us, or betrayed us—can combine to create a ton of pain. But if people wrong us in any way, only we are responsible for how we respond to them. We all need to be aware that anger and bitterness in our lives do not harm anyone but us. In fact, unresolved anger leaves a real mark on our souls, yet I am unsure that we understand how this impacts us and our ability to enjoy our lives.

Anger, bitterness, and hatred can truly enslave us. There is really only one way to be delivered from it, and that is to forgive. However, forgiveness is counterintuitive. To hate is a more natural response when we are hurt or wronged by another.

I have come to realize that if we are not able to forgive, we will have a hard time relinquishing our anger and bitterness. Consequently, we are allowing those who have hurt us to ruin and poison our lives. We are allowing them to steal our joy, and our anger is doing nothing to hurt them.

I love the words of novelist William Young who says, "Forgiveness is for the forgiver to release you from something that will eat you alive, which will destroy your joy, and your ability to love fully and openly."

Is there someone you need to forgive? Remember, forgiveness will liberate you from the past and enable you to live a full and joyful life, now and in the future.

6.6

The Tyranny
of Comparison

A TROUBLING TREND has emerged in our country: a sense of discontentment in people's lives. The root of this issue is that many find themselves trapped in a relentless cycle of comparison. We measure how we are doing by how well we stack up against others.

One of my favorite stories comes from the noted Southern novelist and literary essayist Walker Percy who is known for his peculiar talent in exploring the deeper questions of modern life relating to our habits, our self-deceptiveness, our fears, and our bewildering complexity. In one of his books, a spoof of modern life entitled *Lost in the Cosmos: The Last Self-Help Book*, Percy offers a humorous take on modern Western culture's obsession with pop psychology, which offers simple, untested answers to life's most difficult questions. In the book, Percy gives a battery of multiple-choice tests as a reflection of the self-help quizzes that are so popular in many successful consumer self-help books and magazines. The questions are laced with moral challenges, often highlighted in humorous patterns, one of which I will paraphrase:

> It is early morning and you are standing in front of your home, reading the headlines of the local newspaper. Your neighbor of five years, Charlie, comes out to get

his paper. You look at him sympathetically—he doesn't take good care of himself and you know that he has been having severe chest pains and is facing coronary by-pass surgery. But he is not acting like a cardiac patient this morning!

Over he jogs in his sweat pants, all smiles. He has triple good news! "My chest pains," he crows, "turned out to be nothing more than a hiatal hernia, nothing serious." He has also just gotten word of this great promotion he has received and that he and his family will soon be moving to a new home, which happens to be in a much more exclusive part of town. Then, after a pause, he warbles on, "Now I can afford to buy the lake house we have always dreamed of owning."

Once this news settles in, you respond, "That is great, Charlie. I'm very happy for you."

Now, please fill in the following multiple-choice. There is only one correct answer to each question.

Question: Are you truly happy for Charlie?

   a. Yes, you are thrilled for Charlie; you could not be any happier for him and his family.
   b. If the truth be known, you really don't feel so great about Charlie's news. It's good news for Charlie, certainly, but it's not good news for you.

Percy then gives the following directions:

If your answer to the question above is b, please specify the nature of your dissatisfaction. Do the following thought experiment—which of the following alternative scenarios concerning Charlie would make you feel better?

   a. You go out to get your paper a few days later, and you hear from another neighbor that Charlie has undergone a quadruple coronary bypass and may not make it.

b. Charlie does not have heart trouble, but he did not get his promotion.

c. As the two of you are standing in front of your homes, Charlie has a heart attack, and you save his life by pounding his chest and giving him mouth-to-mouth resuscitation, turning his triple good news into quadruple good news. How happy would that make you?

d. Charlie is dead.

Percy then asks:

Just how much good news about Charlie can you tolerate?

Percy uses this exercise to flesh out the desires of our hearts. He wants to show us how we often compare ourselves to others.

I have concluded that comparison has the tendency to suck the joy out of a person's life. This is so much more problematic today in the world of social media. It is so easy to know who people hang out with, what parties they go to, where they vacation, and what they accomplish in their careers. It has created this incredible fear of missing out.

So what about us? R.C. Sproul says that one sure indicator that a person is healthy and truly content with his life is that when he sees his friends and peers doing well and prospering, he rejoices with them. He is happy for them. On the other hand, when he sees them struggle and go through difficult times, he feels their pain and has great compassion for them. He hurts for them.

Hopefully, this is true of your life, but that is something only you can answer.

6.7

Understanding True Humility

RECENTLY, I finished reading the newly released biography, *Timothy Keller: His Spiritual and Intellectual Formation*. It is a wonderful read.

One morning, I had the opportunity to have coffee with the author, Collin Hansen. I told him that it seems one of the most striking features in Keller's life is his humility. He agreed and said that Keller is humble, quiet, but also very bold. I told him of an old sermon I remembered that Keller had delivered many years ago. In the sermon, he says:

> "The humble are kind and gentle, but also brave and fearless. If you are to be humble, you cannot have one without the other."

I am reminded of a wonderful essay by C.S. Lewis titled, "The Necessity of Chivalry."

Lewis points out how in medieval times, the ideal hero was both humble and kind, yet bold and strong. He references Sir Thomas Malory's book, *Le Morte d'Arthur*, the legendary account of King Arthur and the Knights of the Round Table. In the story, Sir Ector, who raised Lancelot as his son, describes him saying,

> Thou were the meekest man that ever ate in the hall among ladies; and thou were the sternest knight to thy mortal foe that ever put spear in the rest.

Lewis recognized strong dynamic people have this paradoxical blend of being humble and kind, yet brave and fearless. Lewis saw that the medieval ideal required this "double demand" from a knight. In the essay, he says:

> The knight is a man of blood and iron, a man familiar with the sight of smashed faces and the ragged stumps of lopped-off limbs; he is also a demure, almost a maiden-like, guest in hall, a gentle, modest, unobtrusive man.

Lewis says the chivalrous knight has a duality of character in that he is fierce to the nth degree but is meek and humble as well. He believed that the medieval ideal brought these two qualities together even though they "have no natural tendency to gravitate towards one another."

Lewis is right, most modern people greatly desire to be thought of as strong and courageous. To be considered kind and gentle is of little or no importance, particularly to those in the marketplace.

Lewis recognized that the medieval ideal taught humility and restraint to a valiant knight because everyone knew from experience that he needed it. He realized, if it is not possible to produce men who combine the two sides of Lancelot's character, it would not be possible to produce a society with any lasting dignity or happiness.

This reveals the importance and power found in true humility.

7

Wisdom for Character Advancement

7.1

Knowing Yourself

JOHN CALVIN begins his massive work, *Institutes of the Christian Religion* with these words,

> "Nearly all the wisdom we possess, that is to say, true and sound wisdom, consists of two parts: the knowledge of God and of ourselves."

The great philosopher Dallas Willard gives us some good insight into Calvin's words by observing that if you are going to effectively care for something, you have to understand it. This is true of a tomato plant, a rose bush, or a car engine. Willard then says, "If we want to care for our lives, we must understand them."

I remember reading an interview Bob Buford had with Peter Drucker, who was 95 at the time. Drucker is still considered by many to be the greatest management consultant to ever live. He had a great deal of wisdom. In the interview, Drucker says that knowing your strengths and weaknesses is critical if you are going to determine the role you will play in this life. He told Buford, "When you know who you are, you will be comfortable in making decisions about your future."

Drucker then shares an example from his own life. At a certain point in his career, he turned down an incredible offer to become the chief economist at Goldman Sachs. This was an extremely prestigious and visible position that paid a large amount of money. However, Drucker turned them down because he understood his gifts and abilities, and that he could better serve the American business community by developing principles of management and making them useful to companies who would apply them. He recognized that this was his calling in life.

It is so vitally important to know your strengths, your abilities, and what you are passionate about in order to effectively connect with what you are going to do with your life. This includes your retirement years.

It is just as important to recognize your limitations, your flaws, your weaknesses, and your sinfulness. I believe this is crucial, particularly if you desire to change course and walk down the path of wisdom.

A good illustration that demonstrates the importance of this is found in the game of golf. When you are not hitting the ball well and you don't know why, most golfers will take a lesson from a teaching professional. The last time I took a lesson, they filmed me and my swing. They were able to point out the flaws in my swing and I was able to see them very clearly on the video. This enabled me to correct the defects that I was totally unaware of.

In one sense, Jesus confirms this truth. In Mathew 7:3 Jesus points out that we so easily see minor flaws in the lives of others but are blind to the major shortcomings in our own lives. I think this is particularly true in marital relationships. Jesus goes on to say that if we take responsibility for and deal with our own sinfulness, we are able to see others more clearly while being more effective in their lives.

The brilliant French mathematician and philosopher Blaise Pascal once said:

"Truly it is an evil to be full of faults, but it is still a greater evil to be full of them and be unwilling to recognize them."

The ancient Greek philosopher Thales, like all his contemporaries, spoke of the importance of self-knowledge. Yet, he would be the first to point out that it may indeed be the hardest thing to attain. I think when it gets right down to it, so many people are just not willing to take a good, hard look at themselves. They fear what they might discover.

However, if we want to be healthy and care for our lives, we must first understand our lives. But how do we go about this?

I remember many years ago taking the Myers Briggs test. It provides differing psychological preferences in how people see the world. It helps you understand yourself and figure out why you repeatedly stumble into the same self-defeating patterns. One of the most popular self-awareness tests today is called the Enneagram test. I highly recommend it as well.

I should clarify that neither of these tests is all-encompassing, nor do they tell you everything you will ever need to know about yourself. However, they help provide important insight into why people who have the same character traits and personal values are the way they are, as well as their strengths and weaknesses.

For example, I remember a number of years ago, I learned I was an introvert. It was somewhat of a life-changing discovery in that I learned being with large groups for an extended period of time would deplete me. On the other hand, spending time alone would energize me. I did not realize this until I learned I was an introvert.

A second way to better understand yourself is to welcome constructive criticism from others, particularly from your spouse. I think I have learned a great deal about myself from the constructive criticism I have received from my wife. In fact, I suggest whenever you receive any type of criticism that you stop and ask yourself, "Could they be right?"

I recently read that a key feature of wisdom is being in touch with reality and that the one reality that is most crucial to know is who we are. I hope the pages within this book are able to help guide you in this way.

7.2

Impression Management

I WAS recently reading where pop artist Andy Warhol famously prophesied that "in the future, everyone will be world-famous for fifteen minutes." He seemed to anticipate social media as it has turned his prediction into an aspiration of the masses.

Human beings seem to have this unexplained desire for recognition. We want to be noticed by and well thought of by others. Our lives seem to be focused on what John Ortberg calls "impression management." We are consistently seeking ways to impress the world around us so that people believe we are important.

Therefore, so much of what we say and do is intended to impress others. We may casually name-drop, mention our child's accomplishments, or talk about an exotic place where we have vacationed in the past. This happened even back in New Testament times, as Jesus says of the Pharisees, "They do all of their deeds to be noticed by men" (Matthew 23:5).

Sociologist George Herbert Mead explains this principle in a concept called "the generalized other." In our minds, there are certain people on whose judgment we measure our success and failure. Our lives are validated by what they think of us. However, the problem is that we never know in totality what any one person thinks of us.

The philosopher Dallas Willard has written some thoughts on what he calls "the discipline of secrecy." He says we should intentionally abstain from seeking to make our good deeds and qualities known, although it should never involve deceit. He believes we should look to God to enable us to tame our hunger for fame and try to gain the attention of others. Over time, as we practice this discipline, we will learn to embrace anonymity without the loss of our peace, joy, or purpose.

Willard says one of the great tragedies in our lives is holding the belief that all our virtues and accomplishments need to be advertised. We have this deep yearning for them to be known so that we may be celebrated for them. The discipline of secrecy, rightly practiced, enables us to place all our public relations in the hands of God. By doing this, we allow Him to decide when our deeds need to be known. Willard says, "When we desire godly secrecy, our love and humility before God will develop to the point we'll not only see our friends, family, and associates in a better light, but we'll also develop the virtue of desiring their good above our own." Ultimately, we will be content with who we are, rendering what others think of us to be void of meaning.

Back in the 1930s and 1940s, the most popular English novelist was a man by the name of Lloyd C. Douglas. He began his adult life as a Christian pastor and then became a writer.

Five of his books were made into movies. One of the most popular, *The Robe*, was made into a movie, which starred Richard Burton. It won two Academy Awards and was nominated for Best Picture. He also wrote an incredibly popular novel in 1929 entitled *Magnificent Obsession* which was made into a movie, twice. I had the opportunity to read this novel three or four years ago, and it was a fascinating book. (I read that it was one of John Wooden's favorite novels.)

The story is about Dr. Wayne Hudson who is struggling with deep depression and is on the edge of failure in his work. His wife has just died, and he goes to purchase a marker for her grave. As he looks at the various monuments, he encounters an eccentric but very talented sculptor by the name of Clive Randolph. They begin to engage in a conversation, and over time as they become more comfortable with each other, Randolph imparts to him a secret that he claims will transform the doctor's life.

Though Randolph does not completely lay out this wonderful secret all at once, when you piece it together it goes like this. Most people live depleted lives; they are weak, zestless, and have very little energy. The reason, he contends, is that when we perform a good deed or some worthy achievement we want the world to know about it. We seek to advertise it and receive all the credit for it. On the other hand, when our lives are not going well and we are floundering, we carefully hide our problems or look for ways to deny them if we can. Randolph says that people, therefore, spend their lives pretending, always insecure and afraid of being found out.

Randolph tells Dr. Hudson that to remedy this situation and find power in his life, he simply needs to reverse the strategy. In other words, he needed to keep his great deeds and accomplishments a secret and find people with whom he was willing to be vulnerable and share his struggles, fears, and secrets with. After Dr. Hudson began to apply this in his own life, his depression lifted and he later became a famous brain surgeon.

Dr. Hobard Mowrer was a famous American psychologist who was fascinated by this novel, particularly with Randolph's secret formula. Dr. Mowrer decided to conduct some research into the life of Lloyd C. Douglas. He spent time interviewing Douglas's daughter, seeking to determine if her father had actually practiced Clive Randolph's secret formula for power.

Mowrer said it was not surprising "that until he was 50 years old, Douglas was a good but not outstanding minister and then, suddenly, became and remained to the end of his life the most widely read novelist in the English language." Mowrer concluded that if all the facts were known, Lloyd C. Douglas's own life would dramatically testify to the power of this principle which he called "the magnificent obsession."

7.3

What You Do
in Private

I HAVE ALWAYS been fascinated by a person's public life versus their private life. Your outer public life is the part of you that everyone sees. It is visible and, therefore, measurable. It is the part of your life that tells you how well you are doing.

But then you have your private world. Your private thoughts that no one knows about until they become words that come out of your mouth. I have been reading about what we do in private, what we do when no one sees. I do not think we realize how what we do in private can set the course of our lives.

I recently read an article where the author said, "If you want to understand success, you can't focus on what's visible." He goes on to say that:

Nature offers a great example with bamboo, which takes up to 5 years to develop its roots. For years, to the outside observer, no visible progress has been made. Meanwhile, the bamboo grows below the surface, developing its roots and storing energy. Then, all at once, it starts to grow. Years of stored energy result in exponential growth, sometimes reaching over 50 feet in a matter of weeks.

That's how accomplishment comes. Slowly and then all at once.

Everyone wants to experience success, but no one wants to perform the behind-the-scenes work that will get us there.

A highly rigorous scientific study was performed in Berlin in the early nineties. The object of the study was to figure out why some violinists are better than others. The researchers went to the Music Academy of West Berlin as it was known to turn out extremely good musicians, many of whom went on to careers with major symphony orchestras.

Professors were asked to divide their students into three groups. The first group included the very best violinists, the second group was violinists who while good, were not as good as the first group. Those in the third group were good but not as good as those in the first two groups.

The researchers collected a massive amount of biographical data. This included when the musicians started studying music, the competitions they took part in, their success in these competitions, and how many hours a week they had practiced since they started playing the violin.

The subjects were also given a long list of activities, music-related and non-music-related. They were asked how much time they spent on each one in the most recent typical week.

What I found to be most interesting is that the students in all three groups were spending the same total amount of time on music-related activities. This included lessons, practice, classes, and so on. Music activities took up close to fifty hours of their week

However, there was one activity that was clearly more important than any other, and that was practicing by themselves when no one else was around. All the students agreed. When asked to rate the relevance of twelve music-related activities that most contributed to developing their skill, solitary practice was number one. Though all the students knew it, they didn't all do it. The reason, and they all agreed, is that it is hard and it isn't much fun.

I think we should all ask ourselves; how do we spend our surplus hours when nothing is really required of us? Do we invest the time in activities that develop us or do we flitter it away? What do we do with the solitary hours when no one is around, and no one is looking? I close with two famous quotes.

"The heights by great men reached and kept were not attained by sudden flight, but they while their companions slept, were toiling upward in the night."
—Henry Wadsworth Longfellow

"Two roads diverged in the woods, and I took the one less traveled by, and that has made all the difference."
—Robert Frost

7.4

Priorities

I FIRST READ the illustration below in Stephen Covey's book *First Things First.* It is very powerful as it pertains to the priorities of life:

One day this expert was speaking to a group of business students, and, to drive home a point, used an illustration I'm sure those students will never forget.

As this man stood in front of the group of high-powered over-achievers he said, "Okay, time for a quiz." Then he pulled out a one-gallon, wide-mouthed Mason jar and set it on a table in front of him. Then he produced about a dozen fist-sized rocks and carefully placed them, one at a time, into the jar.

When the jar was filled to the top and no more rocks would fit inside, he asked, "Is this jar full?" Everyone in the class said, "Yes." Then he said, "Really?" He reached under the table and pulled out a bucket of gravel. Then he dumped some gravel in and shook the jar causing pieces of gravel to work themselves down into the spaces between the big rocks.

Then he smiled and asked the group once more, "Is the jar full?" By this time the class was onto him. "Probably not," one them answered. "Good!" he replied. And he reached under the table and brought out a bucket of sand. He started dumping the sand in and it went into all the spaces left between the rocks and the gravel. Once more he asked the question, "Is this jar full?"

"No!" the class shouted. Once again he said, "Good!" Then he grabbed a pitcher of water and began to pour it in until the jar was filled to the brim. Then he looked up at the class and asked, "What is the point of this illustration?"

One eager beaver raised his hand and said, "The point is, no matter how full your schedule is, if you try really hard, you can always fit some more things into it!"

"No," the speaker replied, "that's not the point. The truth this illustration teaches us is: If you don't put the big rocks in first, you'll never get them in at all."

The jar is your life. The big rocks are the things that matter most in life, beginning with your most important relationships— God, family, and friends.

The small pebbles are important but not nearly as important as the big rocks. This would include your job, exercise, finances, and reading.

The sand and the water are things in life we enjoy, but in the grand scheme of things are not very important. They are often things that can be quite trivial.

So many people are convinced that to experience a full and happy life, they need to fill the jar with as much as they can. In reality, the jar (your life) can only hold so much.

If you want to live wisely and get the most out of life, you have to prioritize correctly. You have to put the big rocks in first. Most people do not understand this. Instead, they let the gravel, sand, and water become more important than the big rocks.

Unfortunately, we live in a culture that greatly values the trivial pursuits of life (sand and water), and in the process, we easily get carried away by the cultures' priorities. This is why we have to decide in advance, "What comes first in my life?"

As the years go by, this is the only way I know to keep the pain of regret out of our lives.

7.5

Lifetime Learning

OVER TWENTY years ago I was in the insurance brokerage business; for the last ten years, I served as CEO. I remember how my approach to leading the company was to seek continuous improvement. If any company can continuously improve in every area of their business, the financial results will take care of themselves.

In his book, *Discipline is Destiny*, Ryan Holiday validates this approach, particularly when it comes to our individual lives. He describes it as "Get Better Every Day." He quotes Socrates who said, "we cannot remain as we are." Are we growing and improving our lives each day or are we slowly slipping and regressing? We cannot remain the same.

Tom Brady is considered to be the greatest quarterback to ever play football. But what I have learned is that Brady was not obsessed with winning. He was obsessed with the accuracy of his passing, and with getting a little bit faster at releasing the football. He was not willing to remain the same, though it would have been easy to rest on his laurels. The process of getting better is what drove him over the years and that is how he was able to defy aging and all expectations.

The Japanese call this *"kaizen"* which means continual improvement. There is always something to work on, to make a little progress on, with always an opportunity to grow. It starts by finding something to focus on that you can get better at each day. When a person does this, he experiences compounding returns that can be harnessed to produce exceptional results in a person's life.

For me, at this point in my life, my focus is on learning and becoming a better writer. As Charlie Munger said in his commencement address to the class of 2007 graduating from USC Law School:

"It is crucial to be hooked on lifetime learning."

He then references Berkshire Hathaway which he believes is the "best regarded company in the world, with the best investment record in the history of civilization." And, of course, the anchor and leader of this company is Warren Buffet. He says that Buffet spends half of his waking time reading and a big chunk of the rest of his time talking to knowledgeable people all over the world. He says Warren Buffet is "a continuous learning machine."

Munger believes this requirement applies to all walks of life. He says:

"I constantly see people rise in life who are not the smartest, sometimes not even the most diligent. But they are learning machines. They go to bed every night a little wiser than they were that morning. And boy, does that habit help, particularly when you have a long run ahead of you."

What I have noticed is that when a person becomes hooked on lifetime learning, it is noticed by others because it's rare. Therefore, ask yourself, "Will I remain as I am or become what I am capable of?" But please remember, once you stop getting better, there is only one direction to go.

7.6

The Life That
Could Have Been

I HAVE NOTICED a frustration in people's lives that often starts sometime in their 30s and continues on for the rest of their lives. The frustration is over why the gap between the life they have dreamed of and the life they actually end up living.

This reflects what Pulitzer Prize-winning novelist John Cheever said many years ago, "The main emotion of the adult American, who has all the advantages of wealth, education, and culture, is disappointment." Too many adults, particularly as they get toward the end of their lives, experience the awful pain of regret as they reflect on a life that could have been.

There are several reasons this happens in people's lives, (which I outline in my book, *A Life of Excellence.*) but there is one reason that is more of a modern phenomenon. It is what I call "the search for shortcuts."

I recently read that prominent psychologist Martin Seligman said modern people look for shortcuts to find true happiness and it just doesn't work.

Stated differently, many people will tell you their future hopes and dreams, but when it comes right down to it, they do not want to go down the long difficult path to get it. So, they look for shortcuts, believing this can be accomplished through easy formulas and techniques. Examples can be seen in the self-help section of any large bookstore. One will encounter such books as *5 Simple Steps to Double Your Sales*, or *7 Easy Ways to Make Big Money in the Stock Market*. In today's world, if you have a problem, someone likely has a ready formula or technique that claims to help you easily overcome it.

I often see this in counseling people who have pain in their lives. They desire immediate relief. I remember meeting with a man who had been married for a number of years who came to see me because his marriage had unraveled. As he told me his story, it was evident that the marriage was in shambles as a result of the path he and his wife had been on for so many years. The man was a typical Type A personality. He wanted to get things done quickly and was hoping a forty-five-minute counseling session would solve his marital problems. He hoped I might have some type of formula that would untangle the mess they had made of their marriage. I reminded him that it had taken years to get to this low point in his life and there was no quick fix. I then posed the question, "Are you willing to get on a different path, one that may be long and difficult but that will eventually lead to healing, forgiveness, and restoration of your marriage?" He said he was willing.

Dr. Rick Jensen is a nationally recognized sports psychologist whose clients include more than fifty touring pros on the PGA, LPGA, and Champions Tours. Fourteen of his clients have won at least one major championship. He has said that even professional golfers are so often looking for some kind of quick swing fix or putting cure. Jensen comments:

> Golfers don't want to hear that the reason they're not getting any better is because they don't practice, or that their expectations for what it takes to learn and to play good golf are flawed. What they want is to see their swings on video and then saved to a DVD, so they can show their pals what it is they're working on; or they want a quick fix that will cure that slice with minimal effort. Instead, what generally happens is the tip they get doesn't transfer to the course under pressure, and they wind up blaming

their teacher and walking across the street to see another pro. Or they go and buy a book or read a magazine article in hopes of finding a better tip that is the magic pill they're seeking.

Maybe this is why a leading literary critic believes the *Harry Potter* series sold millions of copies. It is full of wish-fulfillment fantasies. The lead character could simply wave a magic wand and instantly make things happen. The critic said, "This is one of the primary fantasies of the human heart." Magic is so much more appealing than painful disciplined effort.

In reality, there is an art to living, and to make progress on life's meaningful objectives, steady plodding along the right path is required. Steady, patient, and often unexciting steps are the most effective way to make substantial progress in life. This doesn't have much appeal to people caught up in our instant-gratification society.

English minister William Carey is a great example of a successful plodder. Despite little formal education, by his teenage years, he could read six different languages. Because of his linguistic skills, he was chosen for an important missionary position in India and later became a professor of Oriental languages at Fort William College in Calcutta. He also founded his own publishing company, which printed Bibles in forty different languages and dialects that were distributed to more than 300 million people.

When Carey was asked how he was able to accomplish so much, he replied that he was a good plodder. In his own words, he said:

> Anything beyond this will be too much. I can plod. That is my only genius. I can persevere in any definite pursuit. To this I owe everything.

If you do not want to reach the end of your life and experience deep regret, you must remember that there is an art to living, and it is not a quick, easy formula. The final outcome of our lives is determined by the paths we go down, and every path has an ultimate, predictable destination.

A second reason we do not achieve the life we dream of is that many of us are not on a quest for truth, growth, and wisdom, but rather on a search for pleasure, fun, and happiness. We are often guided by our feelings and emotions instead of by wise judgment. In other words, our quest for pleasure, fun, and happiness in the now takes priority over sound decision-making that will positively impact our lives in the future.

As one keen observer has noted, people of this world are like children in their approach to life. If you were to offer a child a piece of cake or a $10,000 Treasury bond, he will almost always choose the cake. Children invariably choose immediate gratification without giving consideration to future consequences. They do not understand the value and significance of delayed gratification, yet so many adults seem to be no different. They almost always choose temporary feel-good pleasures over those that have lasting value.

I have concluded that most people do not fully understand the complexity of the human heart and its desires. Have you ever noticed how contradictory your desires can be? For instance, a young man may choose to stay out late partying with his friends, but at the same time, he wants to excel in his career by getting to work early. Notice, there is an obvious conflict in this young man's desires.

Our wants, while endless, are often not in harmony with each other. Modern people seem to gravitate toward those desires that bring pleasure and happiness—like the young man who wants to stay out late with his friends but also wants to excel in his job. Wisdom, however, recognizes the importance of discovering which desires are liberating and which are destructive. Which of my desires are in harmony with who I really am and with what I really desire to do with my life?

One of the most gifted writers ever to live was the English author and poet Oscar Wilde. He was educated in some of Great Britain's finest schools and excelled in the Greek language. His writing earned him great wealth and he was the toast of London. One literary critic described him as "our most quotable writer" after Shakespeare.

Sadly, however, Wilde squandered all that he had and died penniless. Before he died, he reflected on his life and penned these words:

> I must say to myself that I ruined myself, and that nobody great or small can be ruined except by his own hand. ... Terrible as what the world did to me, what I did to myself was far more terrible still.
>
> The gods had given me almost everything. But I let myself be lured into long spells of senseless and sensual ease. I surrounded myself with the smaller natures and the meaner minds. I became the spendthrift of my own genius, and to waste an eternal youth gave me a curious joy. Tired of being on the heights, I deliberately went to the depths in search for new sensation. What the paradox was to me in the sphere of thought, perversity became to me in the sphere of passion. Desire, at the end, was a malady, or a madness, or both. I grew careless of the lives of others. I took pleasure where it pleased me, and passed on. I forgot that every little action of the common day makes or unmakes character, and that therefore what one has done in the secret chamber one has some day to cry aloud on the housetop. I ceased to be lord over myself. I was no longer the captain of my soul, and did not know it.

Wilde desired to live a long life and produce great literary work, but he also loved pleasure. In the end, as he put it himself, "I allowed pleasure to dominate me. I ended in horrible disgrace." Wilde died a broken man at the age of forty-six.

One of our family's mottoes comes from the book *Do Hard Things*. As I tell my children, the path that leads to excellence is often the most difficult, but if we persist in our efforts while going down difficult paths, over time they will become easier. This is not because the nature of the task has changed but because our ability to do it has grown.

My wife provides a good example of this. Though she exercises regularly, she decided several years ago as a personal challenge to take up swimming. The problem is that she did not grow up swimming. The first time she swam laps in the pool, she swallowed a good bit of water. There was nothing enjoyable about the experience; however, she persisted, and over time her swimming improved and the difficult workouts became easier. She has now reached the point where she no longer dreads the pool, but enjoys it, particularly the benefits that come from swimming.

Writer John Piper was correct when he said, "All training is painful and frustrating as you seek to develop certain skills. However, over time, as these skills become second nature, they lead to greater joy."

It is crucial to understand that if we invest time each day in important activities and skill development, we will eventually become very capable. Repetition is the key to enhancing our skills. This is how we build certain habits and disciplines into our lives.

8

Wisdom for a
Life Well-Lived (Legacy)

8.1

The Legacy We Leave Behind

HAVE YOU EVER wondered how your life will be remembered once it is over? What will be the legacy you leave behind?

St. Augustine wrote that thinking and reflecting on legacy is extremely important because it causes us to think maturely about life. In turn, it helps us reconsider who it is we most desire to please.

I do not think we realize how the issue of legacy can change the course of our lives if we are only willing to step back and ask two related questions: How do I want to be remembered? And What do I want my life to have been about once it is over? Peter Drucker, who is considered the greatest business consultant to ever live, said thinking about his legacy early in life is what shaped him so profoundly as an adult.

When I was thirteen, I had an inspiring teacher of religion, who one day went right through the class of boys asking each one, "What do you want to be remembered for?" None of us, of course could give an answer. So, he chuckled and said, "I didn't expect you to be able to answer it. But if you can't answer it by the time you're fifty, you will have wasted your life." We eventually had a sixtieth reunion of that high school class. Most of us were still alive, but we hadn't seen each other since we graduated, and so the talk at first was a little stilted. Then one of the fellows asked, "Do you remember Father Pfliegler and that question?" We all remembered it. And each one said it had made all the difference to him, although they didn't really understand that until they were in their forties.

I'm always asking that question: What do you want to be remembered for? It is a question that induces you to renew yourself, because it pushes you to see yourself as a different person—the person you can become.

Drucker's story proves that once we begin to reflect on how we want to be remembered, it impacts our entire perspective. As we begin to focus on the type of people we are becoming and how our lives are contributing to the lives of others, it will change the way we measure our lives as people. Once it finally dawns on us that we will not be remembered for what we have accomplished, what we have achieved, or even how much money we have made, we acquire the ability to change fundamentally. I think this is what enabled Drucker to turn down Goldman Sachs when he was offered the position to become their chief economist. It was a position that would have paid him a huge salary and thrust him into the international limelight to new heights of fame and glory. But Drucker had a very healthy identity—he knew what he wanted his life to be about, and so he turned them down.

I was reading recently about Charles Dickens and his famous short novel *A Christmas Carol*. Written in 1843, Dickens does a fantastic job showing us how to live a purposeful life and make a difference in the lives of others.

Ebenezer Scrooge's entire life was focused on money and wealth. He cared more about it than anything else in life. In the process, it made him a miserable person that everyone had contempt for. However, as the narrative ends, Scrooge's life is transformed and he becomes focused on using his wealth to benefit the lives of others. His life is now full of joyful purpose, and though this is a work of fiction, how do you think Scrooge would be remembered once his life ended?

I believe as the years go by, we all have a yearning that our earthly lives and endeavors will have some type of permanence that will live on after we are gone.

However, for this to happen, it requires us to be investing in the lives of people. All around us, people are struggling physically, emotionally, and spiritually. Unfortunately, today, so many of us do not want to be troubled by the troubles of others. We do not want our lives to be personally disturbed.

David Brooks believes there is a way to leave a legacy that will help you live better right now. In his wonderful book, *The Road to Character*, Brooks distinguishes between "resume virtues" and "eulogy virtues."

> Resume virtues are professional and oriented toward earthly success. They require comparison with others. Eulogy virtues are ethical and spiritual and require no comparison. Your eulogy virtues are what you really would want people to talk about at your funeral. As in, "He was kind and deeply spiritual," and not, "He had a lot of frequent flier miles."
>
> The striver's life makes it hard to focus on eulogy virtues. We want to be good people, of course, but focusing on eulogy virtues feels just so . . . not special. I have worked my whole career to do something better than everyone else—and I'm supposed to get distracted from that by doing things that anybody can do, like being nice?
>
> But here's the thing. You lose your edge on those resume skills, as everyone either knows or fears. Meanwhile, the eulogy virtues can get stronger and stronger, all the way up the crystallized intelligence curve and beyond. Practiced properly, old people have an edge over younger people, because they have more experience at life and relationships.

Hopefully, we recognize that when our lives are over, we will not be remembered for what we accomplished or how much we accumulated. People will remember us for who we were as people, how well we loved, and the impact we had on others. This is a well-lived life. This is your legacy.

8.2

A Vision for Your Life

PULITZER prize-winning composer Gian Carlo Menotti said, "Hell begins on that day when God grants us a clear vision of all that we might have achieved, of all the gifts we wasted, of all that we might have done that we did not do." No one wants to look back at life and see time and opportunities wasted. That's why it's important to recognize the value of having a vision for your life before too much time passes.

I share this because as I watch people out in the world of business, I have noticed how most of them live reactively rather than proactively. Their lives are little more than a series of reactions to the circumstances they are confronted with each day rather than a proactive life based on a vision of who they are and what they really want to accomplish. They clearly have no real plan or strategy to make life conform to their dreams and their goals. They yearn for a life of significance, yet most do not have the ability and sometimes even the motivation to see beyond their present reality. Few of them have developed a vision for their lives and they just drift along each day.

I first realized the significance of this almost twenty-four years ago as I was considering a career change. I was revisiting Stephen Covey's book, *The Seven Habits of Highly Effective People*, which I had read once before. As I began to look at the second habit—beginning with the end in mind—it was as if a light bulb had finally turned on in my mind.

As we consider our lives and our future plans, we must start with a clear understanding of our ultimate destination. Covey contends the best way to do this is to give serious thought to the legacy we leave behind. He asks us to consider a very effective thought experiment of attending our own funeral:

> As you take a seat and wait for the services to begin, you look at the program in your hand. There are to be four speakers. The first is from your family, immediate and also extended— children, brothers, sisters, nephews, nieces, aunts, uncles, cousins, and grandparents who have come from all over the country to attend. The second speaker is one of your friends, someone who can give a sense of what you were as a person. The third speaker is from your work or profession. And the fourth is from your church or some community organization where you've been involved in service.
>
> Now think deeply. What would you like each of these speakers to say about you and your life? What kind of husband, wife, father, or mother would you like their words to reflect? What kind of son or daughter or cousin? What kind of friend? What kind of working associate?
>
> What character would you like them to have seen in you? What contributions, what achievements would you want them to remember? Look carefully at the people around you. What difference would you like to have made in their lives?

Covey believes this is the foundation that will enable us to develop a vision for our lives (or mission, as he likes to call it). Once we develop a well-thought-out vision, we then can begin to plot a course that will make sure it becomes a reality. Instead of wasting our lives and living reactively, we now have the criteria to measure everything we do in life, including our priorities, our choices, and the use of our time.

8.3

Investing Our Lives

SEVERAL YEARS AGO, a man sent me a wonderful story titled, *It's What You Scatter.* Though I am not certain, I believe it is true. I must tell you, I am touched by it every time I read it. For this reason, I thought I would share it with you.

I was at the corner grocery store buying some early potatoes... I noticed a small boy, delicate of bone and feature, ragged but clean, hungrily appraising a basket of freshly picked green peas.

I paid for my potatoes but was also drawn to the display of fresh green peas.

I am a pushover for creamed peas and new potatoes. Pondering the peas, I couldn't help overhearing the conversation between Mr. Miller (the store owner) and the ragged boy next to me.

'Hello Barry, how are you today?' H'lo, Mr. Miller. Fine, thank ya. Jus' admirin' them peas. They sure look good'

'They are good, Barry. How's your Ma?' 'Fine. Gittin' stronger alla' time.' 'Good. Anything I can help you with?' 'No, Sir. Jus' admirin' them peas.' 'Would you like to take some home?' asked Mr. Miller.

'No, Sir. Got nuthin' to pay for 'em with.' 'Well, what have you to trade me for some of those peas?'

'All I got's my prize marble here.' 'Is that right? Let me see it', said Miller . . . 'Here 'tis. She's a dandy.'

'I can see that. Hmm mmm, only thing is this one is blue and I sort of go for red. Do you have a red one like this at home?' the store owner asked. 'Not zackley but almost.'

'Tell you what. Take this sack of peas home with you and next trip this way let me look at that red marble'. Mr. Miller told the boy. 'Sure will. Thanks Mr. Miller.' Mrs. Miller, who had been standing nearby, came over to help me.

With a smile she said, 'There are two other boys like him in our community, all three are in very poor circumstances. Jim just loves to bargain with them for peas, apples, tomatoes, or whatever. When they come back with their red marbles, and they always do, he decides he doesn't like red after all and he sends them home with a bag of produce for a green marble or an orange one, when they come on their next trip to the store.'

I left the store smiling to myself, impressed with this man. A short time later I moved to Colorado, but I never forgot the story of this man, the boys, and their bartering for marbles.

Several years went by, each more rapid than the previous one. Just recently I had occasion to visit some old friends in that Idaho community and while I was there learned that Mr. Miller had died. They were having his visitation that evening and knowing my friends wanted to go, I agreed to accompany them. Upon arrival at the mortuary, we fell into line to meet the relatives of the deceased and to offer whatever words of comfort we could. Ahead of us in line were three young men. One was in an army uniform and the other two wore nice haircuts, dark suits and white shirts ... all very professional looking.

They approached Mrs. Miller, standing composed and smiling by her husband's casket.

Each of the young men hugged her, kissed her on the cheek, spoke briefly with her and moved on to the casket. Her misty light blue eyes followed them as, one by one; each young man stopped briefly and placed his own warm hand over the cold pale hand in the casket. Each left the mortuary awkwardly, wiping his eyes.

Our turn came to meet Mrs. Miller. I told her who I was and reminded her of the story from those many years ago and what she had told me about her husband's bartering for marbles. With her eyes glistening, she took my hand and led me to the casket.

'Those three young men who just left were the boys I told you about.

They just told me how they appreciated the things Jim 'traded' them. Now, at last, when Jim could not change his mind about color or size . . . they came to pay their debt.'

'We've never had a great deal of the wealth of this world,' she confided, 'but right now, Jim would consider himself the richest man in Idaho...'

With loving gentleness she lifted the lifeless fingers of her deceased husband. Resting underneath were three exquisitely shined red marbles.

Just remember that life is not about how much you accomplish or how much you accumulate. It's about investing in and positively impacting the lives of people in your sphere of influence. This is what you will be best remembered for.

8.4

Our Struggles with Boredom

MODERN TECHNOLOGY brings about change so quickly that the harmful effects are generally not discovered before they are irreversible and before we realize how destructive the effects can be.

Back in the 1960's, the eminent scientist Harlow Shapely wrote on the five factors he believed could potentially destroy Western civilization. The first was nuclear war and terrorism, then famine, climate catastrophe, and a plague or pandemic. The fifth factor he listed was surprisingly, "boredom." He said boredom could destroy us. Shapely believed that "widespread and chronic indifference to ordinary values, pursuits, freedoms, and obligations could lead to our demise, as life becomes absurd and irrelevant.

Fast forward to 1985 when a fascinating book, *Amusing Ourselves to Death*, was written by Neil Postman. This was before the internet and social media, but it is as if he saw it coming. The forward of the book lays out this premise very powerfully.

Postman says everyone was keeping their eye on the year 1984 because of George Orwell's famous book *1984*, a novel about the consequences of a totalitarian government. He modeled the regime in the book after Stalinist Russia and Nazi Germany. It was published in 1949.

But there was another novel that was published just before Orwell's, and just as chilling; Aldous Huxley's, *Brave New World.* Both of these books are about government controlling their people. Postman says:

> Contrary to common belief even among the educated, Huxley and Orwell did not prophesy the same thing. Orwell warns that we will be overcome by an externally imposed oppression. But in Huxley's vision, no Big Brother is required to deprive people of their autonomy, maturity and history. As he saw it, people will come to love their oppression, to adore the technologies that undo their capacity to think.
>
> What Orwell feared were those who would ban books. What Huxley feared was that there would be no reason to ban a book, for there would be no one who wanted to read one. Orwell feared those who would deprive us of information. Huxley feared we would be overloaded with information. Orwell feared Big Brother would conceal the truth from us. Huxley feared the truth would be irrelevant. Orwell feared we would become a captive culture while Huxley feared we would become a trivial culture preoccupied with how we feel.
>
> In *1984*, Huxley added, people are controlled by inflicting pain. In Brave New World, they are controlled by inflicting pleasure. In short, Orwell feared that what we hate will ruin us. Huxley feared that what we love will ruin us.

Here we are seventy years later and it appears Huxley, and not Orwell, was right.

Much has been written about how social media has increased the reality of boredom in people's lives. The reason is that social media offers little challenge, requires little skill, and offers little, if any, reward. Dr. Andrew Lepp says these are the ingredients of a life of boredom.

This, in turn, causes so many who struggle with boredom to seek short-term solutions like electronic entertainment or drugs and alcohol. However, the pleasures of this world are unsustainable and provide only counterfeit fulfillment. This is what leads to spiritual emptiness.

For a life to be well lived, we must focus on the things that truly matter, and I hope this book has helped you gain a better understanding of exactly what those things are. If we do not grasp the importance of constant reflection and seeking out the things in life that will truly bring us joy, peace, and lasting satisfaction, we will likely reach the end of our days and be full of regrets.

8.5

The Pain
of Regret

PRESIDENT JIMMY CARTER has shared a powerful encounter he experienced as a young naval officer; an event that he says shaped his life. To be considered for an officer's position on a nuclear submarine, the candidate first had to be interviewed and approved by Admiral Hyman Rickover, who at the time was head of the United States Nuclear Navy. Here is how President Carter described the interview:

> I had applied for the nuclear submarine program, and Admiral Rickover was interviewing me for the job. It was the first time I met Admiral Rickover, and we sat in a large room by ourselves for more than two hours, and he let me choose any subjects I wished to discuss. Very carefully, I chose those about which I knew most at the time — current events, seamanship, music, literature, naval tactics, electronics, gunnery — and he began to ask me a series of questions of increasing difficulty. In each instance, he soon proved that I knew relatively little about the subject I had chosen. He always looked right into my eyes, and he never smiled. I was saturated with cold sweat. Finally, he asked a question and I thought I could redeem myself. He said, "How did you stand in your class at the Naval Academy?" Since I had completed my soph-

omore year at Georgia Tech before Annapolis as a plebe, I had done very well, and I swelled my chest with pride and answered, "Sir, I stood fifty-ninth in a class of 820!" I sat back to wait for the congratulations—which never came. Instead, the question, "Did you do your best?"

I started to say, "Yes, sir," but I remembered who this was and recalled several of the many times at the Academy when I could have learned more about our allies, our enemies, weapons, strategy, and so forth. I was just human. I finally gulped and said, "No, sir, I didn't always do my best."

He looked at me for a long time, and then turned his chair around to end the interview. He asked one final question, which I have never been able to forget—or to answer. He said, "Why not?"

I sat there for a while, shaken, and slowly left the room.

This encounter caused Carter to completely alter the direction of his life, later inspiring his best-selling book *Why Not the Best?* Admiral Rickover's powerful words to Carter have made me wonder if I have even come close to doing my best in this life, and whether, in reality, anyone ever really does his or her very best? Rickover's final question to Carter seems very pointed and appropriate: "If you have not done your best . . . why not?"

Best-selling author and noted business consultant Stephen Covey takes a slightly different approach to confronting this same issue. He poses a series of questions:

What is the one activity that you know if you did superbly well and consistently would have significant results in your personal life? And what is the one activity that you know if you did superbly well and consistently would have significant positive results in your professional or work life? And if you know these things would make such a significant difference, why are you not doing them right now?

Covey concludes there is one primary reason we seldom pursue these activities: we do not consider them with any real sense of urgency. We most likely recognize that they are important but just not pressing. Therefore we procrastinate, with the justification "I will get to it later."

I am not sure we fully understand that the important activities of life so often don't act on us; we must make clear and conscious choices to act on them. This lack of understanding is perhaps why so many of us spend our lives reacting to the urgent demands of life and then wonder why we're unable to focus on the important activities that will make a significant and lasting difference. As a result, in our day-to-day decision-making, the "urgent" seems to dominate over the "important," and thus we end up with very little personal growth and, at best, a mediocre life.

I believe Covey is right. We have this tendency to drift through life without pursuing meaningful objectives. Research indicates that most people in Western societies do not have a clearly defined strategy or mission for their lives. They live reactively. Their lives become nothing more than a response to the circumstances that are presented to them each day, increasingly in the form of tweets, posts, and emails. Modern people seem to be bound to a frenetic lifestyle, merely doing what is most urgent and immediate.

Too many adults, particularly as they near the end of their time, experience the awful pain of regret as they reflect on a life that could have been. My hope for you is that by the time you reach the end of your life, the pain of regret is nowhere to be found.

9

Spiritual Wisdom

9.1

The Spiritual Dimension of Life

THE BIBLICAL view of human life is that we are all made up of three components—mind, body, and soul.

Another way to think of this is to consider our lives in terms of three dimensions: intellectual, physical, and spiritual.

Prior to the twentieth century, most of Western society saw the importance of making certain that all three of these components were properly nurtured and developed. The prevailing belief was that the spiritual life was of primary importance, followed by the intellect, and then the physical body. This is not to suggest that the care of the body was not important, but reason recognized and acknowledged that the body slows down and deteriorates over time. Meanwhile, the mind and soul have the potential to grow and flourish as time goes by.

Furthermore, the pre-modern world largely accepted the philosophical position that people's lives are generally governed by the health and condition of their souls, which in turn impacts the well-being and quality of their lives.

The more modern perspective on these priorities has changed dramatically. The body and its desires—the sensual side of life—have become of primary importance in modern culture. We have elevated sensuality to the point that it has become the center of our lives, and for so many people it now provides the basic reason for living. Whether it is eating, drinking, pampering our bodies, or sexual activity, the sensual side of life seems to now trump the intellectual and spiritual dimensions. In the process, emphasis on wisdom, character development, virtue, and a life of depth and substance has been swept away. Hedonism prevails.

Of course, the sensual side of life is not inherently bad; in fact, I would contend it is a vital part of the life God intended for His people. Our taste buds, our sexuality, and even restful sleep are all wonderful gifts. The sensual pleasures of life, when enjoyed within boundaries designed by God, can provide great delight. Our sensual experiences are actually an essential part of our humanity.

Apostle Paul shared the important insight that "...we do not lose heart; though outwardly we are wasting away, yet inwardly we are being renewed day by day." (II Corinthians 4:16) Paul was declaring what we all know: our bodies are wasting away each day. However, the good news is that with each new day, we have the opportunity to grow spiritually and to have our souls strengthened and renewed.

It strikes me, however, that so many people believe we are just one-dimensional beings. However, we are clearly more than just a body with physical desires and needs. We have spiritual desires and needs as well. All of us yearn for love, joy, and peace. Although, these are spiritual yearnings that can only be truly satisfied by God Himself.

But do you see what has happened? Humans are attempting to satisfy the spiritual yearnings of the soul with the physical pleasures of life. And it won't work. It can't work. The physical pleasures of life can never satisfy the spiritual longings of the soul.

C.S. Lewis put it this way:

Over the centuries men have tried to invent some sort of happiness for themselves outside of God, apart from God. And out of that hopeless attempt has come nearly all that we call human history – greed, poverty, selfish ambition, war, prostitution, classes, brutal empires, slavery—the long terrible story of man trying to find something other than God that will make him happy.

The reason why it can never succeed in this? God made us and invented us as humans invented the engine. A car is made to run on gasoline, and it would not run properly on anything else. God designed humans to run on Himself. He Himself is the fuel our spirits were designed to burn, the food our spirits were designed to feed on. There is no other. That is why it is just no good asking God to make us happy without bothering to have a relationship with Him. God cannot give us happiness and peace apart from Himself, because it is not there. There is no such thing.

9.2

The Guardian of
Your Soul

I WAS RECENTLY reading some interesting thoughts by Dr. Richard Swenson—a futurist, physician researcher, and very fine author. He believes something is terribly wrong in our land. He calls it a "psychic instability" in people's lives that prevents peace from implanting itself very firmly in the human heart.

Swenson observes that people are frazzled, anxious, and depressed. He says, "this instability is not the same old nemesis recast in a modern role." Something has changed. As people look at the future, there is a fear that grips their heart, and they do not know how to be delivered from it.

Dr. Tim Keller believed this, in some cases, debilitating fear stems from when we have drifted away from our spiritual foundation. He said the beginning of fear is when we conclude we don't need God, because we think we can live a better life without Him. When we do this, we throw the door open for fear to infiltrate our lives.

As we move away from God, we begin to experience a real sense of our own finiteness here on earth. Without realizing it, we are trying to take on a position in the universe that is too big for us to handle. As this begins to happen, we develop a real sense of insecurity and fear begins to creep into our lives.

To understand this sense of insecurity, we need to understand what true security is and where it is found. I love this definition of security, "It is when you build your life on that which cannot be taken away from you." Conversely, insecurity is when you build your life on something that can be taken away from you, and that is our problem.

The key phrase is, "Build your life upon." We should all ask ourselves, "what have I built my life upon?" If it is something that can be taken away from you, then fear will consistently be present in your life.

Augustine said your fears tell you a lot about yourself. He says, "You can always follow your worries to that which you have built your life around."

The highly regarded therapist Rollo May, who was not a Christian, once said, "Anxiety comes when something that you have put your real security in, something that made you feel in control, something that made you feel like you had an identity—is threatened or implodes."

Stephen Covey, in his book, *The Seven Habits of Highly Effective People* nails it when he says we all have a personal center, and whatever is at the center of your life is the source of your security.

The great question of life: is there an ultimate security, a true foundation that we can build our lives on and which will not be taken away from us? The Bible's answer is yes. Christ should be our personal center. He desires for us to walk with Him through life where He guides us, gives us wisdom, and becomes our ultimate security.

A simple way for us to understand this is to see and understand our position in life. God uses great metaphors to help us understand ourselves and our great need for Him.

We are told in the Bible that we as human beings are like sheep. It is the only animal that God compares us to. Sheep are not smart. They will follow one another off of a cliff or into a ditch. They are easily subject to becoming the prey of wild animals or thieves. Sheep are helpless, and God says we are just like them.

For sheep to live, they must have a shepherd. A good shepherd leads, protects, guides, and feeds the sheep. This is his role. However, the shepherd can only fulfill his role if the sheep remain close to Him. When sheep encounter a wild animal or any type of danger, they can rest in the shepherd's care. However, when they go their own way and wander off from the shepherd's care, it is hard for them to rely upon him when a crisis comes along.

All of us are sheep, and Jesus is the good shepherd. If we have never been close to Him or have drifted away from Him, He invites us to come to Him, to draw near. The Apostle Peter describes it like this:

> "For you were continually straying like sheep, but now you have returned to the Shepherd and Guardian of your souls." (1 Peter 2:25)

9.3

The Rabbit That Won't Break Down

HAVE YOU ever wondered why once you have achieved some cherished goal, it does not satisfy you the way you thought it would?

I once read the transcript of the valedictory address given by Kyle Martin at the Kings Academy Prep school in West Palm Beach, Florida. His words were very insightful:

> I stand before you tonight as the 2019 valedictorian. This time last year, I found out that I was in the running for this title. It was then that I decided that I wanted it. So, I worked hard for it. I sacrificed for it and, yes, I stressed for it. And I got it! And, at our senior award ceremony, it felt so good when I heard my name announced with the title. So Good! For about 15 seconds. Yeah. 15 seconds of my heart racing and my adrenaline pumping. 15 seconds of, "Yeah, I won!" 15 seconds of being at the top of the pile of all my accomplishments, and it felt euphoric. But there must come a 16th second. And, on that 16th second, I sat down on my seat, looked at my silver stole that says valedictorian, and I thought, "That's it? What just happened? Why am I not feeling anything else?"
>
> To be honest, I don't even know what I was expecting. A parade of balloons to drop? Or, maybe I was hop-

ing that all my problems would fade away in comparison to this amazing achievement. But none of that happened, not even in my heart. I felt nothing. I was shocked.

I believe Martin's words reflect what so many people experience over the course of their lives. It makes you wonder if everything we have ever thought about finding satisfaction and life's accomplishments is naïve and, possibly, greatly mistaken. I think we end up overestimating the duration of our emotional experience when we achieve our highest goals. It can be incredibly disappointing and quite perplexing.

Philosopher Dallas Willard loved to tell the true story about the dog races in Florida. He says:

> They train these dogs to chase an electric rabbit, and one night the rabbit broke down and the dogs caught it. But they didn't know what to do with it. They were just leaping around, yelping and biting one another, totally confused about what was happening. I think that's a picture of what happens to all sorts of people who catch the rabbit in their life. Whether it's wealth or fame or beauty or a bigger house, or whatever, the prize isn't what they thought it would be. And when they finally get it, they don't know what to do with their lives.

Willard believes this is a major factor in why people find life to be so disappointing. The rabbit they chase does not satisfy. This is why he believed, "We all need a rabbit that won't break down." It must be tied to something that transcends the individual life!

Dr. Tim Keller put it in these words, "If you expect this world to give you happiness, you will be utterly disappointed, because you are asking the world to give you something it cannot give."

These words ring true because the yearning in our innermost being is a spiritual desire of the soul. What we do not seem to realize is that there is a deep thirst in our souls that only God can satisfy.

King David recognized this, which is reflected in his own words from the Psalms:

"For he has satisfied the thirsty soul, and the hungry soul
He has filled with what is good." (Psalm 107:9)

"As the deer pants for the waterbrook, so my soul thirsts for God." (Psalm 42:1)

Psychiatrist Gerald May observed, "After 20 years of listening to the yearnings of people's hearts, I am convinced that human beings have an inborn desire for God. Whether we are consciously religious or not, this desire is our deepest longing and most precious treasure."

This is the rabbit that won't break down.

9.4

Life and Growth

I WONDER if many people stop and evaluate the important areas of their lives, asking themselves if they are growing and developing. If growth is going to happen, we need to be very intentional and proactive about it because life on Earth is impermanent. Everything is constantly deteriorating.

Several years ago, my wife had a little garden in our backyard. She was very attentive to it and it was really a beautiful garden, flourishing under her care. Then, winter came and went and she decided not to pursue the garden in the spring. By late May, her once beautiful garden had become a plot of weeds.

The bottom line is that if you want to see any area of your life deteriorate, just do nothing. Life itself, just the passing of time, leads to decay. This is true in the physical world, and in the world of relationships, but most significantly our spiritual relationship with God.

James Dobson says the natural tendency is for husbands and wives to drift away from each other unless they work at staying together.

To provide an analogy, it is as though they are sitting in separate rowboats on a choppy lake. If they don't paddle vigorously to stay together, one will drift to the north of the lake and the other to the south.

That is exactly what happens when marital partners get too busy or distracted to maintain their love. If they don't take the time for romantic activities and experiences that draw them together, something precious begins to slip away.

It doesn't have to be that way, of course, but the currents of life will separate them unless efforts are made to remain together.

I think it is important to know that there are two types of growth you see in the lives of professing Christians. The first is mechanical growth. It revolves around activities, trying to be religious, and doing your best to live the Christian life. The Pharisees epitomized mechanical growth.

The second type of growth is called organic growth, which is what Jesus desires for His people. While mechanical growth comes through external force, organic growth comes through an important internal power source, the Holy Spirit.

I read of a pastor who was asked by a man if he would be willing to counsel him and his wife. The pastor was told by this man, "My wife is about to leave me. I can't believe it. She has agreed to come to counseling if you will meet with us?" The pastor agrees and they meet. She goes through a list of grievances. She says, "Look, you're domineering. We never mutually come to decisions. You just order me around. Then, you aren't emotionally vulnerable. You never open up to me."

Then, she goes down the list. He looks at her and he says, "Well, I've heard you say these things. I didn't realize they grieved you this much. I didn't realize you were ready to leave me. Of course, I'll change. I will do everything you ask." She says, "Well, all right." Then they go home, and for a while, he changes and does everything she wants.

However, once he is pretty sure she is back to stay, he goes back to his old ways because he is no longer afraid she is going to leave him.

What has happened here? The initial change in the man was mechanical compliance through external force. There was no internal organic transformation.

Jesus gives us a picture of organic growth in John 15, explaining that He is like a vine, we are branches. The sap that flows into the branches of the vine is the Holy Spirit flowing in us. The end result is that the branches bear fruit. This is a picture of organic growth.

The question we must ask ourselves is whether or not organic growth is taking place in our lives. If not, I would remind you again, if you want to see any area of your life deteriorate, just do nothing.

9.5

Is That
All There Is?

IN 1965 one of the most famous rock songs of all time, "(I Can't Get No) Satisfaction" by the Rolling Stones was released. Mick Jagger believed its popularity was due to it being a reflection of the times. Although, I once read where someone said the song actually should have been titled, "I Can't Keep No Satisfaction." We all seem to think we know what will satisfy us. However, once we obtain it, the problem is making that feeling last.

Four years later in 1969, Peggy Lee recorded the song "Is That All There Is?" It was a very unusual song but wildly popular. The woman speaking in the song tells about being taken as a twelve-year-old to the circus that was called "The Greatest Show on Earth," but as she watched, she "had the feeling that something was missing. I don't know what, but when it was over I said to myself, 'Is that all there is to a circus?'" Later she says that she fell "so very much in love" with the "most wonderful boy in the world." Then one day he left her, and she thought she'd die. "But I didn't. And when I didn't, I said to myself, 'Is that all there is to love?'" At every turn, everything that should have delighted and satisfied her did not—nothing was big enough to fill her expectations or desires. There was always something missing, though she never knew what it was. Everything left her asking, "Is that it?"

So every stanza of her life, like a song, went back to the same refrain:

Is that all there is?
Is that all there is?
If that's all there is my friends,
Then let's keep dancing.
Let's break out the booze and have a ball,
if that's all—
there is.

The lack of any deep or lasting satisfaction drives her to joyless partying. As we gradually discover that everything we thought would be fulfilling is not, we become less able to look forward to life, more numb, jaded, and cynical, or worse. The woman speaking in the song realizes her listeners might wonder why she doesn't commit suicide, but she predicts that the experience of dying will be every bit as disappointing as life has been, so there is no reason to hurry it.

The playwright Henrik Ibsen offers some profound insight into this human dilemma. He said, "If you take away the life illusion from an average man, you take away his happiness as well."

A life illusion is the belief that some object or condition will finally bring you the satisfaction for which you long but this is an illusion that, at some point, reality will destroy. In my experience, nothing destroys this illusion like actually achieving your dreams —which might sound a bit confusing at first. What I mean by this is, often, the most disappointing moments in life are when you have just achieved the ultimate and it lets you down.

What we all must realize is that we each have a deep longing in our souls and are searching for something to satisfy this thirst.

I am reminded of the powerful words of the prophet Jeremiah who explains why humans never seem to be able to find the means to quench the deep thirst of their souls. He says:

> "For my people have committed two evils; they have forsaken Me, the fountain of living waters, to make for themselves cisterns, broken cisterns that can hold no water." (2:13)

God tells us He is the source of living water, but so many reject Him, instead seeking to build their own cistern to capture the water that might satisfy the thirst of their souls. However, it is an effort in futility as all human strategies fail us. They are all broken and can not hold water. It leaves us empty.

God invites us to come to the fountain of living water and to drink. There is no other true source for us to drink from.

9.6

The Secret to Life

THERE'S A classic scene in the 1991 movie City Slickers where a father, Mitch (played by Billy Crystal), speaks to his son's elementary school class. After introducing himself and explaining what he does for his job, he delivers this motivational speech:

> Value this time in your life, kids, because this is the time in your life when you still have your choices. It goes by so fast. When you're a teenager, you think you can do anything, and you do. Your twenties are a blur. Your thirties, you raise your family, you make some money, you think to yourself, "What happened to my twenties?" Your forties, you grow a little pot belly, you grow another chin, the music starts to get too loud, one of your old girlfriends from high school becomes a grandmother. In your fifties, you have a minor surgery—you'll call it a "procedure," but it's a surgery. In your sixties, you'll have a major surgery, the music is still loud, but it doesn't matter, because you can't hear it anyway. The seventies, you and the wife retire to Fort Lauderdale, you start eating dinner at two o'clock in the afternoon, you have lunch around ten, breakfast the night before and you spend most of your time wandering around malls looking for

the ultimate soft yogurt and muttering "How come the kids don't call? How come the kids don't call?" In the eighties, you'll have a major stroke; you end up babbling to some Jamaican nurse who your wife can't stand, but who you call mama. Any questions?

The youngsters' eyes grow wider, their jaws dropping, as Mitch drones on about his depressing outlook on life. The message is clear: *It's all downhill from here kids.*

Encouragingly, in the movie, Mitch—in the throes of a somewhat stereotypical midlife crisis—embarks on a mission to recapture a sense of meaning in his life by visiting a dude ranch with friends. During a cattle drive with friends, he meets an older cowboy named Curly. Here's a piece of their famous "one thing" dialogue:

Curly: You know what the secret of life is?
Mitch: No, what?
Curly: (holding up his leather-gloved hand and pointing with his index finger) This.
Mitch: Your finger?
Curly: One thing, just one thing.
Mitch: That's great, but what's the one thing?
Curly: That's what you've got to figure out.

In the end, Mitch discovers that the secret of life isn't a formula; rather, the "one thing" central to living a meaningful life is having strong relationships.

I think we all would agree that life is bankrupt without our human relationships, particularly with those people we are closest to. However, we must know that the most significant relationship in all of life is the one with our God. That is why we are here, to be in a relationship with Him and to live in the center of His will. But what does it mean to be in the center of God's will, and to follow God's will?

What most people don't realize is that God's general will for us is primarily laid out in the Bible. For instance, it is God's will that we are honest, unselfish, generous, and kind. It is God's will that we be faithful to our spouse and that we be humble and forgiving. Living in the center of God's will enables us to live in harmony with what we were designed for and to function well. It lets us live the life we were meant to live. This is the secret to life, this is that "one thing."

9.7

What Will Make Us Happy?

OVER THE LAST one hundred years, America has become more and more secular as people have chosen to live without God. Many still believe in His existence, yet this belief has no real impact on their lives.

Ernest Becker, in his Pulitzer Prize-winning book, *The Denial of Death,* had some interesting words to say about this. Becker was a religious skeptic, but he offers an explanation about the various ways secular people have dealt with this loss of belief in God. He recognized that a loss of belief meant that we are nothing but molecules, we are here by accident and therefore have no sense of a grand purpose for our lives.

So what do we do? He says that we now look to sex and romance to give us the sense of meaning we used to get from faith in God. In describing the modern secular person Becker says:

> He still needed to feel heroic, to know that his life mattered in the scheme of things. ... He still had to merge himself with some higher, self-absorbing meaning, in trust and gratitude ... If he no longer had God, how was he to do this? One of the first ways that occurred to him, was the "romantic solution"... The self-glorification that he needed in his innermost nature he now looked for in the love partner. The love partner becomes the divine

ideal within which to fulfill one's life. All spiritual and moral needs now become focused in one individual . . . In one word, the love object is God ... Man reached for a "thou" when the worldview of the great religious community overseen by God died . . . After all, what is it we want when we elevate the love partner to the position of God? We want redemption—nothing less.

But can a spouse provide the purpose and fulfillment that our souls long for? Becker says no. He goes on to say:

> The failure of romantic love as a solution to human problems is so much a part of modern man's frustration . . . No human relationship can bear the burden of godhood . . . However much we may idealize and idolize him [the love partner], he inevitably reflects earthly decay and imperfection . . . After all, what is it that we want when we elevate the love partner to this position? We want to be rid of our faults, of our feeling of nothingness. We want to be justified, to know our existence has not been in vain.

Now, I do think it is important to point out that marriage is one of God's great gifts to mankind. It can bring incredible joy and delight into our lives. But it can't adequately satisfy us, because that's not how God designed it.

I think Gary Thomas said it best in his wonderful book, *Sacred Marriage:*

> We all enter marriage with the belief that our spouse is going to make us happy—but over time we realize that the ideal relationship we had always dreamed of does not come to pass. Thus we become disillusioned by the inability to receive all the love we believe we should be getting from our spouses. Of course, in this culture which we live, the most popular option in dealing with this disillusionment is to look for a new relationship. We rational-

ize within ourselves and reason that "I just need to find the right person" which translated usually means a new person. However, in a new relationship the same process will inevitably repeat itself—great excitement, the thrill of discovery and then at some point, disillusionment. A new person might look new for a couple of years, they might be shinier with a few less wrinkles, but eventually we discover they had many of the same limitations as the person we traded in. What we fail to realize is that God must be at the center of our hearts and that all our other relationships should flow out of that one central relationship. As odd as this may sound, I have discovered in my own life that my satisfaction or my dissatisfaction with my marriage has far more to do with my relationship with God than it does with my relationship with my wife. Therefore, we should never blame our spouse for the lack of fulfillment, we should blame ourselves for not pursuing more diligently a fulfilling relationship with God.

This is why whenever I am asked to participate in a wedding ceremony or give pre-marital counsel, I emphasize the importance of our spiritual lives and the need to grow spiritually. I explain to each couple that as you deepen your relationship with Christ, He will transform your heart, and this will draw you into a deeper love because you are drawn to each other's hearts.

9.8

Making
a Difference

ONE AFTERNOON, I was having coffee with a man I had not seen in quite some time. The first words out of his mouth were quite unexpected as he asked me, "What kind of problems are you trying to solve?" He obviously was not interested in small talk.

What he was really asking me was "How are you making a difference in people's lives?" Particularly when you consider how so many modern people are lost and experiencing so much pain. It led to a really good conversation.

This reminds me of an article written about a Jewish psychiatrist, Victor Frankl, and his book, *Man's Search For Meaning*. The article spoke of a study performed by a team of psychiatrists who concluded that people today are more interested in finding happiness than meaning. They found happiness is associated with taking while leading a meaningful life corresponds with giving and making an impact on the lives of others.

J.P. Moreland says we should see ourselves in light of a larger cause, or rather, "the outworking of God's plan in history." We should be preoccupied with finding our role in His cause and playing it well. Moreland says we should seek to become the kind of people who can skillfully make those around us better at living their lives.

I think we sometimes forget people are of infinite value.

When C.S. Lewis became a Christian, it changed his entire view of people. Armand Nicholi, who has written on the life of Lewis says:

> Lewis's new worldview changed his valuation of people. Death no longer marked the end of life, but only the end of the first chapter in a book that went on without end. Every human being, he now believed, would live forever —outliving every organization, every state, every civilization on earth. "There are no ordinary people," Lewis reminded his audience in an address given at Oxford.
>
> No one ever talks to "a mere mortal ... it is immortals whom we joke with, work with, marry, snub, and exploit – immortal horrors or everlasting splendors ... your neighbor is the holiest object presented to your sense."
>
> People, in Lewis's new view, transcend in time and significance everything else on earth. This forced him to set new priorities in his life—he first priority given to his relationship with God, the second priority, to his relationship with others.

I think we should also remember when we impact the lives of others, we never know who they may go out and influence. As the Pulitzer Prize historian Henry Adams put it; "A teacher affects eternity, he never knows where his influence ends." Think about how this applies in the spiritual realm, how we truly have the opportunity to participate in the eternal purposes of God.

This reminds me of the movie "t's a Wonderful Life." The great takeaway from the movie is how greatly one life influences another life, and then that life influences another, and so on.

In the movie, an angel named Clarence is attempting to prove to George Bailey how significant his life has been. He does this by showing George what life would have been like in Bedford Falls if George had never existed.

In a very powerful scene, the angel Clarence shows George the grave of his brother Harry. The tombstone reveals that his brother Harry died as a young boy. George protested that it was not true, Harry did not drown that day, because George had saved his life.

The words of Clarence the angel are haunting.

> Clarence: "Your brother, Harry Bailey, broke through the ice and was drowned at the age of nine."
>
> George: "That's a lie! Harry Bailey went to war. He got the Congressional Medal of Honor! He saved the lives of every man on that transport!"
>
> Clarence: "Every man on that transport died. Harry was not there to save them because you weren't there to save Harry."

This is how life works. As Jerry Leachman says, "Life is a generational team effort."

So what are we doing with our lives? Are we making a difference in others that will last over time? Are we investing in endeavors that will live on after we are gone?

One of the most unusual books in the Bible is the book of Ecclesiastes. It is very philosophical and thought-provoking. The author of the book, (who most people believe is King Solomon), speaks of the incredible wealth he has built up, the experience of every pleasure known to man, the knowledge he has gained, and all kinds of beautiful building projects he completed during his life. In the end, he experiences a deep sense of emptiness. He describes his life as vanity, like chasing after the wind. All that he experienced and accomplished was in vain.

Is there anything I can do with my life that is not vanity, that is not done in vain? Yes! The Apostle Paul put it in these words:

"Be steadfast, immovable, always abounding in the work of the Lord knowing your toil is not in vain in the Lord." (1 Corinthians 15:58)

9.9

The Greatest Cause of Misery in Our World

C.S. LEWIS is considered by many to be one of the greatest authors of all time. More than 300 million copies of his books have been sold; and though he died in 1963, hundreds of thousands of his books are still purchased each year. One of his most well-known works is *Mere Christianity*, in which he intellectually lays out a defense of the Christian faith. In a section labeled "Christian Behavior," he discusses topics such as cardinal virtues, social and sexual morality, forgiveness, charity, and hope, followed by a chapter entitled, "The Great Sin."

Lewis reveals that the great sin in life is pride and arrogance. He explains that this is because "Pride has been the chief cause of misery in every nation and every family since the world began."

Lewis goes on to describe pride as a spiritual cancer, destroying our ability to genuinely love others and preventing us from being content. As a spiritual cancer, pride slowly grows and develops in our lives, becoming well-established without our knowledge. Lewis says pride is purely spiritual; it originates straight from hell and, consequently, is far more subtle and deadly than all other sins. We readily recognize it and hate it in others, but most of us believe that we are in no way afflicted by it.

Without realizing it, pride explains so much of the dysfunction in our lives:

1. It explains why we worry so much about what people think about us.
2. It explains why we always compare ourselves with others.
3. Pride keeps us, particularly men, from having good relationships—we can't be transparent. We can't share our struggles, our weakness, our fears.
4. It explains why we are paralyzed by the fear of failure—which is like a psychological death.
5. And then when we do experience any type of failure: experience great shame—which for many leads to depression and often suicide.

There truly is a dark side to pride, one that is extremely difficult to see. Sociologist Anthony Campolo shares how this so often plays out with parents in the raising of their children:

> We will never know how many children's lives are made miserable by being pushed to achievements solely to make their parents look good. Children who are driven to psychological exhaustion for academic achievement often know their labor is primarily to enhance the status of their parents. Behind the parents' claims of simply expecting their children to do well because success in school will increase their options, the ugly reality is that the achievements of the children visibly demonstrate the superiority of the parents. This is what pride can do to our families.

A few years ago, I had the opportunity to watch Ken Burns' fascinating documentary on the Vietnam War, as well as the movie "The Post" which is about the Pentagon Papers.

When it became apparent that the Vietnam War was not winnable and that the United States should pull out, 85% of our military leaders refused to endorse this option because they felt it would be humiliating. Their pride would not allow them to go along with this decision.

Lyndon Johnson refused to pull out because, as he put it: "I would not look very manly." If we chose to withdraw our troops Richard Nixon made a similar response: "I do not want to be the first president in history to have lost a war."

This is what pride can do to a nation. Thousands of young men died in Vietnam because of the pride of our leaders. All because prideful leaders feared that withdrawing from a war, even one they knew was not winnable, would be a bad look.

This has made me wonder what the ultimate extent of pride's devastation is to people's lives and relationships. Its consequences can cascade through our lives. It creates incredible instability, fear, and weakness. Since we cannot detect pride in the depths of our hearts, we never really know what is wrong with us.

This is why humility is of great value. Stephen Covey said, "Humility truly is the mother of all virtues. It makes us a vessel, a vehicle, an agent instead of 'the source' or the principle. Humility is the place of growth and strength. There is power in the humble life.

9.10

Thanksgiving Therapy for the Soul

IF YOU LOOK closely, you will notice a historical pattern in Western civilization. God blesses certain people who are hard-working, but who are also humble and thankful and depend on Him in their day-to-day living. Over time, they experience a certain degree of abundance and wealth.

After time passes, these people slowly begin to take credit for all of their prosperity. Their hearts turn to pride and they forget about God. Finally, they descend the slippery slope into the abyss.

In the Old Testament, Moses said arrogance is looking at your life, your abilities, and your achievements and thinking, in your heart, it is your strength, your power, and your ability that has led to all of your success. Humility helps you to recognize that all you are and all you have is a gift from God and a result of other people contributing to your life.

In his book, *The Case for Character*, Drayton Nabers provides remarkable insight into the humble life, saying, "...humility is a form of wisdom. It is thinking clearly. It is simply being realistic. It is knowing who really deserves the credit and the glory for what we do."

There is a wonderful true story along these same lines in Stephen K. Scott's inspiration, *The Richest Man Who Ever Lived:*

My former church pastor, Dr. Jim Borror, while visiting a church in the Northwest, was asked by a woman to meet with her husband, a multimillionaire entrepreneur with thousands of employees. Although this man had tens of millions of dollars and everything money could buy, he was unhappy, bitter, and cantankerous. No one liked being around him, and contention and strife followed him wherever he went. He was disliked by his employees and even his children. His wife barely tolerated him.

When he met the man, Dr. Borror listened to him talk about his accomplishments and quickly realized that pride ruled this man's heart and mind. He claimed he had single-handedly built his company from scratch. Even his parents hadn't given him a dime. He had worked his way through college.

Jim said, "So you did everything by yourself."
"Yep," the man replied.
Jim repeated, "No one ever gave you anything."
"Nothing!"

So, Jim asked, "Who changed your diapers? Who fed you as a baby? Who taught you how to read and write? Who gave you jobs that enabled you to work your way through college? Who gave you your first job after college? Who serves food in your company's cafeteria? Who cleans the toilets in your company's restrooms?" The man hung his head in shame. Moments later, with tears in his eyes, he said, "Now that I think about it, I haven't accomplished anything by myself. Without the kindness and efforts of others, I probably wouldn't have anything." Jim nodded and asked, "Don't you think they deserve a little thanks?"

That man's heart was transformed, seemingly overnight. In the months that followed, he wrote thank-you letters to every person he could think of who had made a contribution to his life. He wrote thank-you notes to every one of his 3,000 employees. He not only felt a deep sense of gratitude, he began to treat everyone around him with respect and appreciation.

When Dr. Borror visited him a year or two later, he could hardly recognize him. Happiness and peace had replaced the anger and contention in his heart. He looked years younger. His employees loved him for treating them with the honor and respect that true humility engenders.

From this, it should strike us all that humble people are grateful people. They give thanks to those who deserve the credit rather than claiming it for themselves. Therefore, through practicing thankfulness we humble ourselves and acknowledge that all we are and all we have is a gift from God.

What I have come to realize is that thanksgiving does not come naturally to human beings because we like to take credit for everything that comes into our lives.

Therefore, a grateful heart is something that has to be cultivated. Like with all other habits, if you are truly going to cultivate a grateful heart, you have to be intentional about it. It is something you have to plan to do every day. Author Henri Nouwen once said,

> In the past, I always thought of gratitude as a spontaneous response to the awareness of gifts received, but now I realize that gratitude can also be lived as a discipline. The discipline of gratitude is the explicit effort to acknowledge that all I am and have is given to me as a gift of love, a gift to be celebrated with joy.

Every morning, I spend the first ten to fifteen minutes of the day giving thanks to God. I start by acknowledging all that I am and all that I have is a gift from Him and that I am grateful. I thank Him for the gift of life and for a new day. I thank Him for my health and for keeping me in this life (Psalm 66:9). I thank Him for my wife and our life together as well as for our three children. I thank Him for the other relationships He has blessed me with. I thank Him for our home and the financial resources He has provided us. I thank Him for the work He has called me to do and for the talents and abilities he has blessed me with. I give thanks for all the spiritual blessings of life (Ephesians 1:3). Finally, I end by thanking Him for the incredible difference He has made in my life. Where would I be without Him?

I am convinced that intentionally taking time to thank God daily has made a profound difference in my life. Over time, I have noticed it leading me to give thanks throughout the day as I recognize His good hand in all I do. I have come to realize this not only pleases Him, but it has also transformed my life.

This should not be surprising when you consider the research of Dr. Hans Selye, an Austrian-Canadian endocrinologist who died in 1982. Selye was among the first scientists to discover the impact emotions have on a person's health. During his life, he wrote thirty books on the subject of stress and human emotion. At the end of his life, he summarized his research, concluding that a heart of gratitude is the single most nourishing response leading to good health. Selye believed that thanksgiving and gratitude are therapy for the soul, and a healthy soul benefits physical health.

As I was researching thanksgiving and gratitude, I discovered two recent articles that presented sound arguments on how gratitude has such a powerful impact on our lives. The first article was "How Gratitude Influences Loving Behavior" from *Psychology Today*, and the second was "Thanksgiving and Gratitude: The Science of Happier Holidays" from *The Wall Street Journal*. The authors of these pieces relied on scientific research to come to their conclusions. What we learn from them is:

1. *Gratitude* is the foundation of satisfying relationships. There is nothing more deadly than when people in a loving relationship feel taken for granted.
2. *Gratitude* expresses appreciation. Human interaction flourishes when people feel appreciated.

3. People who are the most materialistic in our culture are very ungrateful and extremely unhappy. Materialism and gratitude have an inverse relationship; ungrateful people are clearly unhappy people.

4. *Gratitude* acknowledges all the great benefits of life and enables us to savor all that is good in our lives.

5. Finally, and it should come as no surprise, a thankful heart is associated with a number of positive health benefits. Grateful people have stronger immune systems, report fewer symptoms of illness, and enjoy a better quality of sleep. They are also less reactive to stressful events.

Thanksgiving begins with the recognition of who really deserves the credit and glory for what we do. It is most pleasing to God but it also does something to us. It is life-giving and transformative. Gratitude is where the path of wisdom begins. It is like therapy for the soul.

10

Final Reflection

10.1

Final Reflection

AS YOU HAVE READ this book, I hope you have realized there is truly an art to living well, and the foundation is wisdom. Modern people do not seem to value wisdom the way past generations did, but I hope you see that it gives you a true interpretation of the world and how we should live in it. To lack wisdom is to be without direction and to be lost in a world that does not make sense.

Scholar Neal Plantinga reveals that the correct order of life is wisdom. He then gives us great insight into the value of wisdom when he explains that wisdom is "finding out the truth about what life is, what makes the world work, and how we ought to fit into it."

This explains why wisdom is of such abundant value. It not only gives coherence to life but provides a path leading to our ultimate well-being and happiness. As you finish this book, you should stop and ask yourself, "What is this worth to me?"

Acknowledgments

I AM first and foremost grateful to all of my family, friends, and colleagues here at The Center for Executive Leadership who have encouraged me along the way as I have worked on this project. Most significantly, I want to thank Caroline Bates who has worked tirelessly to see this book become a reality.

I would be remiss if I did not acknowledge individuals whose work greatly influenced the substance of this book. Primarily Tim Keller, whose work has profoundly shaped my thinking and perspective on the issue of "wisdom."

Finally, as with any writing, I acknowledge that I am standing on the shoulders of those who have come before me. I offer my deep appreciation to the many people whose writing has informed this work.

About the Author

RICHARD E. SIMMONS III is the founding director of The Center for Executive Leadership, a faith-based ministry he started in 2001 in Birmingham, Alabama, focused on counseling businessmen and professionals.

Richard is a best-selling author of *The True Measure of a Man*. His approach is structured and methodical, and his passion is transforming lives through gaining wisdom and applying truth to every area of life.

Richard was born and raised in Birmingham, Alabama, and educated at Sewanee, The University of the South. He worked in the insurance industry for 28 years before starting The Center. When he's not spending time with his family, he enjoys teaching, counseling, writing, or speaking to men's groups across the country. Follow Richard on social media and listen to Reliable Truth on your favorite podcast app.

richardesimmons3.com | Follow Richard on

ALSO BY RICHARD E. SIMMONS III

All books are available from our website:
richardesimmons3.com

THE REASON FOR LIFE
Why Did God Put Me Here

Why was I born? Why am I living? In this book I seek to answer these questions recognizing that if there is a God out there, why did he put me here? What is the reason for my earthly existence? I hope the insight in this book might enable you to understand what is the reason for life.

A LIFE OF EXCELLENCE - GRADUATION EDITION
Wisdom for Effective Living

For the graduate in your life. *A Life of Excellence* lays out three principles that clearly point to a life of excellence. I am convinced that if one lives in accordance with these principles, their life will flourish and prosper.

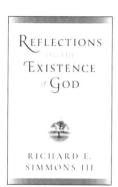

REFLECTIONS ON THE EXISTENCE OF GOD
A Series of Essays

This book is a series of short essays seeking to answer life's most enduring question: Does God exist? I have attempted to craft a book that is well researched but also easy to read and understand. Each essay can be read in less than 10 minutes.

In the end it is important to know whether God exists or He does not exist. There is no third option. What I am seeking to do in this book is to determine which of these beliefs is true and which one is not.

COLLEGE WITH NO REGRETS
Wisdom for the Journey

College is one of the most exciting and meaningful times in life. However, for all the exciting things college offers, it may bring big questions—perhaps even some fear or anxiety. This book will make you wiser and equip you to better navigate your own journey through the college experience.

THE POWER OF A HUMBLE LIFE
Quiet Strength in an Age of Arrogance

This book examines what I consider to be life's greatest paradox — that strength is found in humility.

WISDOM: LIFE'S GREAT TREASURE
Timeless Essays on the Art of Intentional Living

A collection of short essays on wisdom to serve as a guide to help people walk in wisdom on their journey towards a healthy and meaningful life.

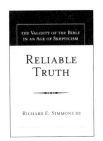

RELIABLE TRUTH
The Validity of the Bible in an Age of Skepticism

Do you believe the Bible is the inspired word of God? *Reliable Truth* offers powerful and compelling evidence why the Bible is valid and true.

A LIFE OF EXCELLENCE
Wisdom for Effective Living

A Life of Excellence lays out three principles that clearly point to a life of excellence. I am convinced that if one lives in accordance with these principles, their life will flourish and prosper.

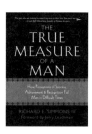

THE TRUE MEASURE OF A MAN
How Perceptions of Success, Achievement & Recognition Fail Men in Difficult Times

In our performance-driven culture this book provides liberating truth on how to be set free from the fear of failure, comparing ourselves to others and the false ideas we have about masculinity.

RICHARD E. SIMMONS III

SEX AT FIRST SIGHT
Understanding the Modern Hookup Culture

This book explains the hookup culture–how it came about, how it is affecting our younger generation and finally, God's intent for our sexuality.

REMEMBERING THE FORGOTTEN GOD
The Search for Truth in the Modern World

A fresh, contemporary approach to Christianity, a compassionate yet forceful statement of personal belief.